"The church is a family, and as with any family, there are bound to be disagreements. In a world of increasing theological relativism and shifting political correctness, there's plenty to get upset about. This much-needed book is a practical guide to picking your battles and developing the art of loving people with whom you disagree. Muehlhoff and Langer demonstrate that we can do both—and must for the health of the church."

Andy Steiger, president of Apologetics Canada

"Much of my work is in the realm of ethnic unity, where people hold very deep convictions and many times say the wrong thing. Sadly, when this happens, they are met not with grace and civility but with meanness. And most of this work is among Christians! We need to reexamine what we hold dear and how we can communicate our beliefs in a way that's winsome and compelling. For this I'm grateful to God for Tim Muehlhoff and Richard Langer and their timely resource, *Winsome Conviction.*"

Bryan Loritts, teaching pastor at the Summit Church in Raleigh-Durham, author of *The Dad Difference*

"It's hard to imagine a more timely and relevant book for the church today as we navigate faithful living in a post-truth, post-civil, pandemic culture where the church seems as divided as the rest of the country. Muehlhoff and Langer spotlight the pivotal role that the church's transformational ministry can have during such times, and how it can lead the way in witnessing Christ in hospitable ways to a weary and often fear-filled public. These thoughtful scholars and practitioners prod us patiently, persistently, and gently to understand how we can experience Christian unity and what's at stake. A must-read."

Robert H. Woods Jr., professor of communication and executive director of the Christianity and Communication Studies Network

"It's no secret that when followers of Christ disagree, we often emulate the divisive approaches modeled for us by popular influencers of our day. I'm grateful for Tim Muehlhoff and Rick Langer's groundbreaking work that is piercingly relevant for this cultural moment. Finally, a book that excavates oft-forgotten biblical principles about disagreeing, and challenges readers to consider relationship over being right. It's a well-researched work that plumbs the depths of the topic more than most while remaining personal and practical. This book is refreshingly counterintuitive and is a rallying cry for the bride of Christ to be an attractive representation of disagreeing with listening, compassion, and understanding rather than giving away influence through divisive means."

Brian Mount, COO of Hume Lake Christian Camps, cofounder of Bridge Conciliation

"After ministering in the nation's capital for forty years, it is our conviction that this inability of believers to thoughtfully disagree and to carefully hear and understand the strongly held beliefs of others who see things differently is a shameful reality that must be acknowledged and overcome. The time is now. Muehlhoff and Langer have given us a wise and practical tool that can help all of us—especially in our churches."

John and Susan Yates, The Falls Church Anglican, Falls Church, Virginia

"Our culture seems to be increasingly defined by sharper elbows or sharper edges or sharper tongues. This seems antithetical to the gospel, which calls for truth with grace and grace with truth. The polarization evident in politics, media, and universities is even showing up in the church. Polarizing attitudes are not unifying attitudes, and this must grieve the heart of God. Through this book, Biola professors Rick Langer and Tim Muehlhoff offer a timely, helpful, and hopeful resource for Christians who yearn to cultivate biblical kindness and unity as we together seek truth. This thoughtful and practical book will certainly go a long way to help Christians model healthy discourse around crucial issues and to reclaim a winsome gospel witness to a broken world. I would put this on a must-read list for any Christian today who is a leader or aspiring to lead."

Barry H. Corey, president of Biola University and author of *Love Kindness: Discover the Power of a Forgotten Christian Virtue*

"This book could help us turn this world right-side up with meaningful conversations filled with kindness, grace, truth, and welcome. If you're tired of debating and the ensuing division, here's an alternative to change the conversation!"

Sharon A. Hersh, licensed professional counselor and author of *Belonging: Finding the Way Back to One Another*

"The passion of Rick Langer and Tim Muehlhoff is to 'find ways to deepen our beliefs and convictions while preserving the unity of the Spirit and the bond of peace.' And they mean it. Helping us to understand where our own convictions come from—and are they absolutes or merely preferences?—is the starting point. Beyond that, they give us a backpack full of journey tools with which to undertake winsome conversations, reconciliation conversations, educating and edifying conversations. A must-read for the Jesus follower who cares about truth and biblical community and how they must intersect, particularly in our combative, vitriolic times."

Jenni Key, shepherd of prayer at Fullerton Free Church, chair of the Evangelical Free Church of America board of directors

"As a shepherd, I can't think of a more urgent and pressing need among disciples of the Lord Jesus today than the tools discussed in *Winsome Conviction*. My heart aches for the widespread pursuit of the 'wisdom from above' described in James 3 that is 'first pure, then peaceable, gentle, open to reason, full of mercy and good fruits, impartial, and sincere'; this book shines a light upon that pathway to peace among Christians who disagree. Muehlhoff and Langer have essentially laid out a battle plan against our enemy the devil in his most obvious attack in this age."

Darin McWatters, lead shepherd of Fullerton Free Church, Fullerton, California

"If you've been in a disagreement with a fellow believer that disintegrated into quarreling, you need this book. All over our world today we see Christians quarreling—in the church, on social media, and anywhere else opinions can be shared. And the volume on these disagreements seems to be getting louder. How do we disagree yet still resemble the Lord? In this timely book, Tim Muehlhoff and Richard Langer give practical steps for sharing our convictions in a way that still allows for unity."

Katie Potesta, community group pastor at the Fullerton Free Church, Fullerton, California

"The body of Christ historically argues over issues. This treatise strikes a remarkable balance between scholarly treatment of biblical text, historic examples, and down-to-earth common sense to give twenty-first-century Christians counsel in navigating the landmines of culture, politics, and theology when they sit down to commune at the foot of the cross. Well done and extremely helpful!"

Steve Highfill, district superintendent of the EFCA West, retired, and church consultant

"This is a book people have literally been asking for. How can fellow Christians—pursuing truth and bound by grace—arrive at such divergent conclusions on matters of enormous significance? Rather than becoming resigned to endure bitter discord with those whom we are called to love— or worse, ignoring them completely and retreating to safe echo chambers— many are ready for a more productive way to honestly explore and passionately express our deepest beliefs while still honoring the *imago Dei* of our fellow pilgrims. It is time for the way of winsome conviction."

Brian J. Shook, chief of staff at Biola University

WINSOME
CONVICTION

DISAGREEING WITHOUT
DIVIDING THE CHURCH

TIM MUEHLHOFF *AND*
RICHARD LANGER

An imprint of InterVarsity Press
Downers Grove, Illinois

InterVarsity Press
P.O. Box 1400, Downers Grove, IL 60515-1426
ivpress.com
email@ivpress.com

*InterVarsity Press® is the book-publishing division of InterVarsity Christian Fellowship/USA®,
a movement of students and faculty active on campus at hundreds of universities, colleges, and schools
of nursing in the United States of America, and a member movement of the International Fellowship
of Evangelical Students. For information about local and regional activities, visit intervarsity.org.*

*All Scripture quotations, unless otherwise indicated, are taken from The Holy Bible, New International
Version®, NIV®. Copyright © 1973, 1978, 1984, 2011 by Biblica, Inc.™ Used by permission
of Zondervan. All rights reserved worldwide. www.zondervan.com. The "NIV" and "New International
Version" are trademarks registered in the United States Patent and Trademark Office by Biblica, Inc.™*

*While any stories in this book are true, some names and identifying information may have been changed
to protect the privacy of individuals.*

Cover design and image composite: David Fassett
Interior design: Jeanna Wiggins
Image: © IkonStudio / iStock / Getty Images Plus

ISBN 978-0-8308-4799-0 (print)
ISBN 978-0-8308-4800-3 (digital)

Printed in the United States of America ♾

*InterVarsity Press is committed to ecological stewardship and to the conservation of natural resources in all
our operations. This book was printed using sustainably sourced paper.*

Library of Congress Cataloging-in-Publication Data
A catalog record for this book is available from the Library of Congress.

P	25	24	23	22	21	20	19	18	17	16	15	14	13	12	11	10	9	8	7	6	5	4	3	2	1
Y	37	36	35	34	33	32	31	30	29	28	27	26	25	24	23	22	21	20							

To three individuals who've shaped my thinking about communication: J. P. Moreland for giving me a vision for strategic cultural engagement; Tim Downs who—through the Communication Center—provided encouragement and confidence to work out my thoughts; Julia T. Wood who selflessly continues to share a lifetime of expertise and passion.

—Tim Muehlhoff

To the members of the countless small groups of which I have been a part—in the early years of my Christian discipleship, in my many years of vocational ministry as a pastor, and in my more recent years as a university professor. These groups, whether Bible studies, reading groups, or boards, have taught me to savor the taste of a love that is deeper than our disagreements.

—Richard Langer

CONTENTS

INTRODUCTION

CHRISTIAN UNITY IN
THE ARGUMENT CULTURE

"Trump Should Be Removed from Office."

"I won't feed into this mass hysteria, nor scare my own children by wearing a mask!"

"Sure, racism exists, but the idea of systemic racism is fake news!"

Each quote is a different iteration of the beginning of this book. We were looking for current controversies in which believers have opposite opinions. They each see their position as a Christian conviction so they expect all Christians to share it. As soon as we picked one issue, it was pushed aside by another.

"Trump Should Be Removed from Office" is the title of *Christianity Today*'s then editor-in-chief Mark Galli's controversial op-ed piece where he argues that the president has abused his power for personal gain and should be impeached. He concludes by asking if sincere Christians can honestly continue to assert that "the bent and broken character of our nation's leader doesn't really matter in the end?"[1] Clearly many Christians shared Galli's opinion since after the essay appeared, subscriptions to *Christianity Today* increased. On the other hand, two hundred evangelical leaders publicly slammed the op-ed, claiming it "questioned the spiritual integrity of Christians."[2] It seemed like the perfect example of conflicting Christian convictions. That is, until COVID-19 hit.

"I won't feed into this mass hysteria, nor scare my own children by wearing a mask!" This was exclaimed by a participant in a Zoom meeting of local church leaders gathering to discuss how to respond to the pandemic. The topic of wearing a facemask dominated the discussion and provoked powerful disagreements. While each sought to fulfill the second great commandment, they had vastly different ideas of what that meant in practice. To one side, neighbor love is not perpetuating—via wearing a mask—an overreaction that is only stoking needless fear. To the other, loving our neighbors means showing deference to those in our community who are fearful and adopting precautions advocated by reputable health experts. With a deadline approaching, this introduction seemed even more relevant.

But while the ink was drying on that draft, we all witnessed the horrifying killing of George Floyd whose cries of "I can't breathe" fell on the deaf ears of a White policeman with a knee on his neck. "I can't breathe" became the rallying cry of protest marches across the world pushing COVID-19 to the background. In the midst of the swirling controversy, a pastor friend of ours angrily asserted, "Sure, racism exists, but the idea of systemic racism is fake news!" He represented conversations being held in hushed tones in predominately White churches across America. Racism exists, of course, but systemic racism is not supported by the facts. Sorry. Such views deeply hurt many Christians and especially Christians of color who felt ignored, again.

What all three quotes have in common are not only powerful emotions but deep divisions among Jesus followers. This division wasn't started by calls for impeachment, a pandemic, or Black Lives Matter protests. Cracks in our unity were already present. These challenging events simply brought them front and center where they can no longer be ignored. The truth is that any attempts to follow Jesus often lead sincere Christians in different and seemingly incompatible directions.

Can you relate?

While your disagreement with a person sitting in the pew in front of you or a Christian colleague at an organization or school may not concern something as dramatic as impeaching a president or defunding the police, we all know what it's like to be angry and disappointed with the convictions of a fellow believer.

By the time you read this introduction, there may be something new dominating the headlines and pulling Christians apart. The question is, what can be done?

The only thing more difficult than discussing Christian convictions in the public square is discussing them with fellow believers in the church. This may seem counterintuitive but it is true. We may have *more* disagreements with nonbelievers, but our disagreements with fellow believers are more problematic and more emotionally charged.

Outside the Christian community, one anticipates having biblical convictions contested or despised. Disagreement is unpleasant but expected. We know our beliefs about Christ and morality are not broadly shared in the American public square. Therefore, we expect conflict and are equipped for it—or at the very least know we should be. But when our personal convictions are contested by fellow church members, everything changes. We feel attacked from behind. It feels both unexpected and wrong! We assume our biblical convictions will be shared by those sitting on either side of us in church. If they doubt or deny our convictions, we don't experience it as a mere difference of opinion but rather as a violation of an unspoken agreement. We are not merely intellectually challenged by a new idea or puzzled by a different viewpoint; we are hurt and offended.

This offense is not unique to the American church. As we have traveled internationally, we've heard the same concerns coming from church leaders in Canada, Indonesia, Kenya, Uganda, Korea, Lithuania, Russia, China, Romania, and England. It seems the challenges to Christian unity are experienced worldwide, and this isn't merely a modern struggle fueled by social media. Paul tells believers at Corinth that they have been called to be holy "together with all those everywhere who call on the name of our Lord Jesus Christ" (1 Cor 1:2). Yet, nine verses later he writes that he has learned there are "quarrels among you" (1:11).

Why is this? We believe one of the main causes of discord is how we think about our convictions. Consider these three commonly held beliefs.

1. Strongly held convictions lead to uncivil discourse. The reason we fight with each other, and often believe the worst about each other, is that we form convictions about things for which we care deeply. Unfortunately, we all care deeply about different things. And even when we care about the same things, we often see these things differently and therefore commit to different courses of action. If we are going to live together, we will need to moderate our convictions. We need to learn to say "Whatever" more and "Thus saith the Lord" less.

2. Convictions are about moral absolutes. Simply put, as we walk through life, we encounter two types of issues: absolutes and preferences. It is important that we distinguish these two. If something is merely a preference, we should just live and let live and not argue about it. We can't argue about it. A preference is just a matter of taste. How can you argue that chocolate is better than vanilla? You can't really give reasons for that sort of thing. On the other hand, there are absolutes. These are moral issues—issues of right and wrong. We should form convictions about these issues, and we should follow our convictions even when we don't feel like it, even if it is difficult or unpleasant. So, convictions are what we have about absolutes, and preferences are what we have about matters of taste.

3. Christians should all share the same convictions. We understand that the world may have different (and mistaken) views about absolutes since they do not share a commitment to the authority of Scripture. Christians, however, share a commitment to the authority of Scripture and therefore should share the same absolutes. Since convictions are about absolutes, and we all share the same absolutes, all Christians should share the same convictions. In practice, of course, we may have disagreements about convictions because we are fallen and sinful, but clearly God's intention is that we should all agree.

We wrote this book to explain why each of these three beliefs about convictions is *wrong*. To give a preview where the book will be going, let's sketch our reasons for rejecting each of these three claims.

First, we do not believe that strong convictions cause incivility. Instead, we believe poorly formed convictions cause incivility. In fact, what is really important about a conviction is not whether it is strong or weak but rather whether it is well-formed or poorly formed. So, we'll discuss how convictions are formed and how to form them well.

Second, we will dispute the claim that convictions are about absolutes. To put it more precisely, we will dispute the claim that the Christian life confronts us with only two types of issues: absolutes and mere preferences. Perhaps the single most important point we will make is that contemporary Christians need to reexamine and recover the realm of "disputable matters," a realm Paul examines in some detail in Romans 14.

Third, we do not believe that all Christians will agree on all matters of conviction. Once we have identified the third ground of disputable matters, we realize that many of our convictions are not about moral absolutes. Therefore, even if we are optimistic enough to assume that all Christians share the same moral absolutes because they read the same Scripture, there is no particular reason to assume they will share the same personal convictions. Some of our convictions are formed on disputable matters—matters that all Christians within a church may not agree on. God wants us to form a conviction on such matters, but he does not want us to force such convictions upon others.

It is clear, then, that we cannot expect the church to be free from the sorts of division we find within our culture. The line of contentious conversations does not just run between the church and the world, it runs right through the heart of every congregation.

OUR JOURNEYS

Tim. Long before I became a professor, I was part of a unique Christian think tank sponsored by Cru (formerly Campus Crusade for Christ). The goal was to consider ways we could share the Christian perspective—seen by many as argumentative and harsh—in a way that balanced truth telling with love. My work with this group piqued an interest in communication, and I soon started my graduate education at UNC-Chapel Hill. There I met brilliant scholars who introduced me to the topic of civility, which culminated in the development of an original four-step method of bringing together groups locked in disagreement marked by incivility, lack of compassion, and vitriol. This idea of cultivating civility has been a recurring theme found in many of my books.[3]

On separate occasions over the past few years, I found myself in the unexpected position of serving as interim teaching pastor at two churches in Southern California. It's there I had the chance to see firsthand how Christians can both foster unity amidst disagreements and also how those different points of view can form deep divisions. My admiration for Christian leaders who seek to engage differences—rather than sweep them away or suppress them—has grown immensely.

Rick. The first two decades of my ministry experience were spent serving on the pastoral staff of what became a large evangelical church in Southern California, and it didn't take long for me to realize that conflicts were part of church life. I experienced everything from family squabbles brought into the church by warring siblings all the way up to challenges to unity that struck the highest levels of our church leadership. During this time, I also served on the board of the Southwest District of the Evangelical Free Church and on the board of Forest Home Christian Camp and on community boards as well. After twenty years at my church, I joined the faculty of Biola University and continue to teach and serve in leadership there to the present day. These roles gave me wide-ranging experience in conflict resolution with Christian churches, boards, universities, and organizations. My interest in fostering civil discourse has also extended outside of Christian circles, and I have volunteered for the past few years with Better Angels as a moderator for workshops that bring together right- and left-leaning citizens to discuss their conflicting political convictions.

Since Tim and I met upon joining the faculty of Biola University, we've not only become friends and co-authors but were tasked by our school president to cultivate dialogue among diverse faculty who find themselves on opposite ends politically and theologically. We call these conversations *faculty duologues* and have tackled questions such as, Is capitalism biblical? How should our biblical convictions influence how we vote? Does social justice detract from the gospel, or is it the heart of it? These are public conversations held in front of fellow faculty, the student body, and the general public. The lessons we've learned—both successes and failures—have shaped our thinking and approach. Our desire to cultivate civil conversations not only resulted in the book you are about to read but the creation of the Winsome Conviction Project (WCP). The WCP is a five-year project built on the idea that in today's argument culture the value of listening, compassion, and understanding have been largely discarded. Our vision statement reads: *Our vision is to foster conversations within the church and the broader culture that deepen relationships, help to heal a fractured church, foster civility, bring compassion to a warring public square, and enrich the lives of listeners rather than tear people apart.*

As the toxic polarization and division that characterizes contemporary culture creeps (or floods) into the church, it's not enough to merely consider the formation of convictions. We must also learn how to have productive conversations about our convictions. How do conflicts form and take on momentum? How do we form impressions of other Christians, and are these impressions accurate and charitable? Are the groups we belong to within a church or Christian organization open to outside input, or are they echo chambers fostering closedness and groupthink? And last, how should the biblical virtues of respect, humility, and love play in how we not only form convictions but also communicate them?

SECTION I

BIBLICAL
FOUNDATIONS

1

HISTORICAL PRELUDE

ROGER WILLIAMS

It is January of 1636. A solitary figure trudges through the New England snow as the pale midwinter sunlight is slowly swallowed by the dusk. It is bitter cold already, and it will surely become colder as night descends. The figure is not hurrying home for the night. He has no home. He does not look forward to being greeted by his wife and children because his pregnant wife and two-year-old daughter are trudging through the snow a short distance behind him—doing their best to keep up as he seeks a place to shelter for the night.

Who is this pitiable figure, and what circumstances have led him into this desperate plight? Is he a victim of a natural disaster—a winter storm that destroyed his home? Was his home destroyed by pirates, hostile Indians, or a rampaging criminal band? Is he a criminal who chose exile rather than execution?

The answer is none of these.

The solitary figure is Roger Williams. He and his small family have not been banished for a crime but rather banished for their convictions. They are not risking the snow in the hopes of preserving their lives; they are risking their lives in the hopes of preserving their consciences. As Williams put it, he was determined to keep his soul undefiled by refusing to "act with a doubting conscience."[1]

Roger Williams may be best remembered as the founder of Rhode Island (the final destination of his trudge through the frozen woods), but he was also a pioneer of the separation of church and state—something he viewed as necessary to allow people to preserve their consciences intact. He was a man of complex thought, controversial opinions, and deeply held convictions. If he were alive today, he would share many characteristics with conservative evangelicals (or perhaps fundamentalists), particularly in these early years we describe here. He was absolutely committed to the lordship of Christ and expressed that commitment by absolute obedience to God's Word. He believed in the literal return of Christ and expected it at any time. He was personally committed to evangelizing the indigenous population in the "wilderness," but he was also convinced that many of the English settlers were also unregenerate and in desperate need of repentance and conversion. He was deeply committed to the purity of the church, wanting membership in the church to be dependent on a clear testimony of faith in Christ, and he was also firmly committed to church discipline, including excommunication for those whose life and practice gave the lie to their profession of faith.

Williams's Christian beliefs were also his final authority and guiding light when it came to controversial issues like politics. Though he was prone to withdrawal and separation on matters of church polity, he was very much engaged in the broader society and very concerned about civic and political matters. It was not long before this pastor and missionary was serving as the civil governor of the colony that grew up around the settlement he began near what is now Providence, Rhode Island.

Roger Williams has excellent street cred as a Christian of radical commitment. But what is truly interesting is the convictions that emerged from his devoutly held faith. Let us modernize Williams's positions by setting them within more contemporary controversies to see what we would think about them. In all likelihood, Roger Williams would have been:

- adamantly opposed to viewing America as a Christian nation. He would have felt that was untrue as a matter of historical fact, but he also would have opposed making this a goal or aspiration as a matter of principle;
- opposed to including the phrase "under God" in the Pledge of Allegiance;
- opposed to prayer in public schools; and
- opposed to using religious symbols like the cross in public places and swearing in ceremonies for juries or public offices that included the Bible or oaths in God's name.

So, easy come, easy go when it comes to street cred for many contemporary conservative evangelicals.

What accounts for the radical difference between the political convictions of Roger Williams and so many modern evangelicals? It turns out the difference has almost nothing to do with time and historical context. In fact, John Cotton, the Boston pastor who was instrumental in sending Williams into his bone-chilling exile, would have disagreed with him at every point mentioned above, though he shared almost all of Williams's confessional beliefs.

Surprised? Confused? We were too when we first read about Roger Williams. Let's look a little deeper into his beliefs.

Let's begin by making a theological point that was very important to Roger Williams. For most of New England's Puritans, "covenant" constituted a sort of canopy under which all of human society operated. Husbands and wives were united in a marriage covenant, local churches organized around covenants which included professions of faith and commitments to holy living, and society itself ultimately stood in a covenant with God as well.[2] For Williams, this covenant canopy was misconceived. Civil society was a mixed society in the sense that it was not all made up of Christians—as was clearly shown by requiring confessions of faith to join a local church. If society was universally Christian, this would be a pointless exercise. But if society was mixed, how could it stand in a single covenant before God? How could it require certain beliefs for participation in civil society? The fact that civil society was impure and mixed necessitated a division between church and state.

Williams was firmly convinced that the New Testament church is strictly spiritual and entirely distinct from any civil body. In light of this, he made a strong contrast between Israel, which was a political nation, and the church, which is not and never will be. Historian Edwin Gaustad clearly explains: "New England was still hung up on Moses [and] refused to accept that there really is a New Testament, a new covenant, a new dispensation. . . . The New Israel is the Christian community, spiritual alone, not physical. Under the dispensation of the gospel, *nations are not churches.*"[3]

This belief makes Williams's surprising convictions much easier to understand. For him, neither America nor any other nation could properly lay claim to the term "Christian" in describing itself. Another consequence of being a mixed society is that all public positions and civic responsibilities will be discharged by both Christians and non-Christians. Therefore, oath-taking for civil service (be it on a jury or to hold office) is inappropriate. In effect, it requires a person who does not believe in God to invoke the name of God in an oath. This is a violation of the command not to take God's name in vain and also of Jesus' teaching in the Sermon on the Mount regarding oath-taking (Mt 5:33-37). Therefore, it is not a stretch to assume that for Williams, if the Pledge of Allegiance is to be recited by all citizens, it should not invoke God's name—on the lips of unbelievers, God's name would be devoid of any spiritual meaning. In fact, this is made explicit in Supreme Court Justice Sandra Day O'Connor's defense of the words "under God" in the Pledge. She finds the phrase is not unconstitutional "because it serves a legitimate secular purpose of solemnizing public occasions, and expressing confidence in the future."[4] But wouldn't this mean precisely that God's name is being used in a sense that is devoid of any meaningful theological content? Isn't this the very definition of using God's name in vain? Similar thinking would likely forbid teacher-led prayer in public schools since they hire both Christian and non-Christian teachers. How could they sincerely offer prayer in Jesus' name, and why would you want teachers praying in any other name?

Such concerns may also apply to matters like the public display of the cross or other Christian symbols, but at this point, the story gets even more interesting. The English flag of the colonial era contained a red cross which formed its axis. It had been bestowed upon England by the pope some centuries before. To Williams this was another vestige of Christendom—and worse yet it came clothed in explicitly "popish garb." Therefore, Williams became an ardent supporter of John Endecott, the leader of the Salem congregation, who ordered the crosses cut out of the flags.[5]

This story has a particular resonance for me (Rick). For many years I pastored in Redlands, California, a small town on the far eastern edge of the Los Angeles basin. In 1963, the city created a logo for its stationery, business cards, and government buildings and vehicles. The logo had four quadrants, one of which contained a cross glistening above a steepled church, representing the fact that Redlands was known as a community with an unusually high number of churches. Though commonly called the "city seal," it was really just a logo. In 2004, the American Civil Liberties Union (ACLU) wrote a letter requesting that the cross be removed on the basis of the separation of church and state. The city council complied with the request and began removing the offending logo. Christians strenuously objected by organizing through various churches, schools, and organizations. I was approached by several other pastors and asked to rally our church to the cause. The Christian legal group known as the Alliance Defense Fund offered to plead the case. Ultimately, a ballot initiative to restore the city seal was rejected by approximately 60 percent of the voters, and the city reverted to its pre-1963 seal.

What would Roger Williams have thought? Interestingly enough, the city initially responded by putting black tape over the offending portion of the logo and even drilling holes in badges of police officers to remove the cross. At the time, I could hardly help but be reminded of Roger Williams and John Endecott cutting the crosses out of the flags of New England. The irony is that in Williams's day the cross removal was being done by the conservative Christians rather than the ACLU.

What should we make of all of this? First, I think Roger Williams serves as a great example of the point we made in the introduction: all Christians do not share the same convictions on all issues. More importantly, we don't have different convictions because some Christians are devout and others are merely nominal in their faith. Roger Williams was far more devout and zealous than most of us who make up evangelical churches today, myself included. (I'm sure I would have come up with some way to salve my conscience and avoid tromping through the snow with my two-year-old and my pregnant wife.) Williams is a great example of devotion, but he is also an ominous warning of the dangers of division. He left in his wake a collection of church splits and divisive tracts with names like *The Bloudy Tenent of Persecution for Cause of Conscience,* and *The Bloudy Tenent yet more Bloudy by Mr. Cotton's Endeavor to wash it white in the Blood of the Lamb.* John Winthrop, the first governor of the Massachusetts colony, said that Williams at one point had refused Communion with all save his own wife.[6] John Cotton accused him of rejecting as apostate every church in the New World (as well as the Old).[7]

We have a lot to learn from Roger Williams about personal devotion, but he also serves as a cautionary tale about dividing the body of Christ. We hope his story will whet your appetite and prod you to think more closely about what convictions really are and how we can hold them firmly but without dividing our churches and destroying our friendships.

2

DISPUTABLE MATTERS

THE FORGOTTEN MIDDLE GROUND

What is the greatest threat to the church of Jesus Christ today?

There are so many threats to choose from. Some Christians would identify hazards like postmodern relativism working to unravel notions of truth and the rise of the LGBTQ agenda, intending to turn traditional sexual norms on their head. For others, the great threats to the church look different. Other Christians feel our most existential threat is the inability to achieve racial justice, or our refusal to confront sexual predators within the clergy, or sexism within our culture. At a global level, relentless persecution and the rise of Islamic fundamentalism threaten the lives of individual Christians and the very existence of the church.

But without denying the significance of any of these threats, we believe the greatest threat to the church today is the same as it has been in every generation since the New Testament was written: quarreling. Persecution strengthens the church. Intellectual and cultural challenges deepen our faith and stimulate our theological thinking. Ethical commitments that conflict with the culture make us stand out as salt and light—or at times may provoke us to purify our own lives to become better salt and light. Quarreling, on the other hand, is insidiously dangerous because it kills from within.

The existential threat of quarreling leaps from the text of almost every New Testament epistle. Whether the letter is long or short (1 Corinthians or Philemon), quarreling is addressed. Whether the church is doing well or doing poorly (Philippians or Galatians), quarreling is addressed. Whether the tenor of the epistle is doctrinal (Romans) or personal (2 Timothy), quarreling is addressed. Clearly, the New Testament views this type of discord as a life-threatening virus, a metastasizing cancer set on destroying its host.

In Paul's day the church quarreled over the Jewish law and over genealogies, over meat sacrificed to idols and sabbath practices, and over favoritism shown to the rich patrons and negligence shown to poor widows. Churches clashed over the incarnation and the resurrection. They fought over which apostle was better than the others. They butted heads over race, class, and gender. They quarreled over the Spirit of Peace.

Modern churches are no different. We did some searching in the World Christian Database.[1] Our query for Lutheran denominations yielded 186 distinct records worldwide. That sounds like a lot, but the Methodists (including Wesleyans) recorded 301 entries, only to be bested by the Reformed denominations (including Presbyterians) with 311. Yet it appears no one could beat the Baptists, who pegged the needle at 472, though it is possible that number is inflated if the Reformed Baptist denominations were counted twice.

Or consider the Mennonites.[2] They are an Anabaptist church, distinguished among other things by the practice of baptizing only adult believers. Though united on baptism, Mennonites found things a bit harder when it came to Communion. Questions arose over including foot-washing, exchanging holy kisses, and having love feasts. All resulted in church divisions. Controversies also arose over using ordained versus lay ministers and then over the style of colonial coat that a minister should wear. A division arose over the keeping of written minutes and the use of written constitutions in churches.

Churches split over whether worship should take place in houses or churches. All agreed that young men who were drafted should not serve in the military, but division arose over whether young men could do public service or if they were required to go to prison when drafted. Divisions occurred between those who used automobiles and those who used horse-drawn buggies, and over whether or not automobiles should have chrome bumpers or black bumpers. A division arose over farming with tractors rather than horse teams, soon followed by a division among tractor drivers as to whether steel wheels were required or if rubber wheels were permissible. There was division over the necessity of head coverings for women and whether head coverings should be bonnets or hats. All of these controversies led to splits between groups of churches, new formal and informal alliances, and a variety of splinter denominations. Perhaps none of this should be surprising. One of the earliest Mennonite conflicts was over "shunning"—in effect, it was a division over the proper way to divide.

My own denomination, the Evangelical Free Church, was proud of our simple one-sentence doctrinal statement in the early twentieth century. We were able to bridge the gap over baptismal practices and include congregations that practiced both infant baptism and believer's baptism. This wonderful unity almost unraveled in the 1920s when some churches wanted to publish the denominational newsletter in English rather than Swedish.

Fortunately, since quarreling is as old as the apostles, we are also given apostolic wisdom to help manage this problem. Many passages in the New Testament address quarreling, and one of the most complete and most instructive is found in Romans 14. Let's consider that passage in some detail and see if it offers us a way forward that works even in our contested world today.

PERSONAL CONVICTIONS
AND CONGREGATIONAL QUARRELS

In Romans 14, Paul broaches a painful disagreement within the congregation over convictions about days and diets. Some members of the church felt that Christian freedom meant that a person could eat anything they wanted to and that all days were essentially alike. Others disagreed, believing that what one ate and how one ate it was spiritually significant, and likewise, they felt that some days were sacred and should be particularly honored in comparison to others.

A word of caution for modern readers: this is *not* a discussion about trivial matters. The Roman church consisted of a mix of Jews and Gentiles. Questions about the relationship between Jews and Gentiles permeate almost every chapter of the book. Given this context, few matters could be more contentious than days and diets. Keeping the Sabbath and practicing the dietary laws were the two most common and readily visible ways in which devout Jews proclaimed their allegiance to Yahweh. It was both a tangible expression of their identity as the people of God and also a way to avoid contamination in a pagan world where food, especially meat, was often part of ritual sacrifices. Days and diets were anything but trivial to Jewish Christians in Rome.

The same is true in the Gospels. The Jews challenge Jesus concerning what he is eating, who he is eating with, or what he is doing on a Sabbath day. Though Jesus claimed he did not come to abolish the law, many devout Jews felt he was abolishing the law exactly because of how he dealt with days and diets. Clearly, when Paul picked up the thread of days and diets toward the end of Romans, he was choosing a very thorny and contentious issue for his readers—*not* an easy question or a trivial disagreement.

With this in mind, let's examine the wisdom Paul passes along to the Roman church about dealing with conflicting personal convictions. Four key principles can be drawn from this chapter.

Principle 1: Distinguish personal convictions from moral absolutes and matters of taste.

As for the one who is weak in faith, welcome him, but not to quarrel over opinions. One person believes he may eat anything, while the weak person eats only vegetables. Let not the one who eats despise the one who abstains, and let not the one who abstains pass judgment on the one who eats, for God has welcomed him. Who are you to pass judgment on the servant of another? It is before his own master that he stands or falls. And he will be upheld, for the Lord is able to make him stand. (Rom 14:1-4 ESV)

Paul begins this chapter by identifying the matters that are appropriate for forming personal convictions. Paul is addressing matters of "opinion" or "disputable matters" depending upon the translation. Apparently, some matters are disputable and others are not. This statement merits further attention.

Not everything is a disputable matter. Some things are matters of absolutes. Absolutes include matters like the incarnation, the resurrection, and the deity of Christ. New Testament writers offer clear teaching on these matters and also clearly identify and condemn false teaching—often in the strongest of terms. These are not matters of personal convictions; these are matters of universal belief within the church. The exact formulation of these doctrines developed over time and were ultimately codified into great definitional statements of faith—statements we know to and recite today under names like the Apostles' Creed or Nicene Creed. We could call these "Christian convictions" since, by definition, those who do not share these convictions are outside the church.

There are also absolutes related to conduct rather than belief. For example, in the immediately preceding passage (Rom 13:12-14), Paul commands all of his readers to cast off the works of darkness, meaning that they should not engage in drunkenness and orgies and sexual immorality. Putting on Christ, according to Paul, demands that one make no provision for the flesh. This is not merely a personal matter because Paul thinks every member of the church should share this moral mandate. In other words, it is a moral absolute, not a matter of *personal* conviction. There is no room for disagreement here.

On the other hand, some matters do not merit dispute at all. They are fundamentally not important. They are matters of taste, accidents of history, or mere differences. In Romans 12:3-12, for example, Paul discusses the different spiritual gifts and argues that differences among them should not lead us to think differently about ourselves. All gifts should be valued equally—they are equally good; they are equally gifts. There is no reason for dispute regarding gifts. Perhaps more relevant is Paul's exhortation to the Corinthians (1 Cor 1:11-5; 3:3-7) who were quarreling about who had baptized them and over which apostle had led them to Christ. Paul is horrified that this has become a disputable matter for them. He states that it does not matter who baptized a person but that they were baptized into Christ. It doesn't matter whose preaching brought you into the church; what matters is that that person was preaching Christ. One's preacher and one's baptizer are matters of mere difference or accidents of time and place. They are not worthy of dispute. They may be personal matters, but they are not matters of personal *conviction*.

So, when Paul identifies *disputable matters*, he introduces a third category between moral absolutes and mere differences. He is pointing to matters where Christians can legitimately disagree regarding what is right or wrong. And make no mistake, these truly are contentious matters—either because brothers and sisters in Christ will judge right and wrong differently, or because one Christian views the issue as a matter of right and wrong and the other views the issue as a mere difference. So even the categories can be disputed. Such issues are disputable matters, and these matters are the focus of Paul's attention in Romans 14.

One more bit of terminology needs to be clarified. Paul mentions the "one who is weak in faith" and contrasts this person's conscience with that of a person who is apparently stronger in faith. What is surprising is that Paul uses the labels weak and strong in almost exactly the opposite fashion than they are commonly used today. Paul identifies the one who is weaker as the one who has a robust or even *hyperactive* conscience—he or she has tighter self-imposed prohibitions on conduct than the one who is stronger. The person who has a weaker faith has a hard time believing that dietary laws and Sabbath laws are actually past and superseded by the coming of Christ. This person feels safer continuing to honor these laws because of the sensitivity of their conscience.

Being "weak" in faith does not call into question the authenticity of one's saving faith in Christ. Romans 14 assumes saving faith is in place for all the individuals Paul is addressing. Rather, in this passage "faith" refers to the firmness of one's belief that a particular course of action is appropriate and pleasing to God. As renowned biblical scholar F. F. Bruce notes, "He who has doubts is condemned, if he eats. If he does something about which his conscience is uneasy, he is condemned at heart and incurs a sense of guilt, 'because his action does not arise from his conviction' (NEB). But one who does something knowing it to be not only permissible but positively right does it from faith."[3]

What Paul has in mind here is not our saving faith in Christ but rather faith that a particular believer has in the merits of a particular course of action. This sort of faith will vary between believers depending on the course of action. A person who is "weaker" in faith is not really sure that eating meat is permitted. The one who is "stronger" in faith feels full Christian liberty to eat without raising a question of conscience. If a different activity were under consideration, the labels of weak and strong might be reversed. A person who has a particularly sensitive conscience about drinking might have relatively few scruples about watching movies, while a person who is very concerned about watching movies might be unconcerned about drinking. So the labels weak and strong apply to particular issues of conscience and not to a person taken as a whole, and they are not the equivalent of being spiritually mature or immature.

Furthermore, the reason why a person may have a particularly robust or even hyperactive conscience on a particular issue can vary quite widely. In the case of Romans 14, the believers in question were probably either Jewish believers (or perhaps god-fearing Gentiles sensitized to the Jewish law) who from their earliest days had been trained to eat only certain types of food and to honor particular days in a special way. Their personal history of religious devotion sensitized them to days and diets. But all of us have histories, and with these histories come our own sensitivities. A friend of mine refuses even to taste alcohol because he was an alcoholic for many years. He now celebrates his "sobriety day" the way most of us celebrate our birthdays. His conscience is sensitized because of a personal history of excess and sin related to alcohol. Another friend, a pastor of a large church, refuses to go to any R-rated movies, including movies like *The Passion of the Christ*, because he is concerned that it will start him down a slippery slope into watching films with ever more violence or sexuality, something he knows himself to be drawn to. The sensitivity of a person's conscience may come from one's religious background, from a history of personal sin, or from a desire to safeguard against a personal weakness or inclination of soul. In any case, Paul exhorts us to honor our own consciences in these matters and to be sensitive to the consciences of others. Even if we have no temptation toward excess in drinking and feel free to partake in drinking alcohol, we are not to flaunt our freedom before a brother or sister who does have sensitivities in this regard.

With these clarifications in place, let's consider the remaining principles Paul offers to guide us in forming personal convictions about disputable matters.

Principle 2: Don't quarrel. Paul began this passage by commanding his readers to avoid quarreling over disputable matters. This seems paradoxical—isn't *disputable* just a synonym for something we quarrel about? Paul's response to this is straightforward. When he calls something a disputable matter, he simply means that it is a matter about which good-hearted believers can disagree. One person can have one opinion, and the other person can have another opinion, and that is that. There is no need to reconcile their beliefs with one another. And since there is no need to reconcile the beliefs with one another, there is no need to quarrel. We do not have to figure out who is right and who is wrong. There is room for two opinions. End of story.

It is worth noting that Paul does not even claim all viewpoints are equally valid. In fact, in the matter of days and diets, he implies the weaker brother may actually be further from the mark. As he puts it: "I know and am persuaded in the Lord Jesus that nothing is unclean in itself, but it is unclean for anyone who thinks it unclean" (Rom 14:14 ESV). Nonetheless, the weaker faith should be welcomed by the stronger faith, and likewise, the person with the weaker faith should not judge the person with the stronger faith. In Paul's mind, I should be able to choose my belief in such matters, and you should be able to choose your belief. Since we are both free to choose, we are also free to differ.

On the surface, this seems fairly unsurprising, but it is easy to mistakenly infer that Paul is telling us that disputable matters are no big deal, just matters of taste. But this completely misses Paul's point. Although disputable matters are not absolutes, they are also *not* matters of taste or of mere difference. Disputable matters are a middle ground, and it turns out they are exactly the ground in which personal convictions are grown.

Principle 3: Be fully convinced in your own mind. In verses 3-6, Paul explicitly debunks the notion that we can avoid controversies on disputable matters by essentially saying, "Who cares? Whatever." Though Paul does not want us to judge each other, he still believes these matters are too important to just make a choice and get on with it. In verse 5 he says, "Each one should be fully convinced in his own mind" (ESV), and in verse 12 he reminds us that "each of us will give an account of himself to God" (ESV). Paul also talks about his own convictions regarding food and states that he knows and is persuaded of them (v. 14). In verse 23 he reminds us that "whatever does not proceed from faith is sin" (ESV). This is strong language. Paul clearly wants his readers to carefully think through disputable matters and resolve any residual doubt. To those who ask, "Who cares?" Paul replies, "Jesus cares!" The reason we don't judge each other on these matters is that we will each be judged by Jesus (v. 10). Each person must prayerfully consider whether each day is alike or whether some days are special; whether all food is permissible or whether some must be avoided. They will not answer to other believers about these matters, but they will answer to God.

Paul is asking his readers to develop *personal convictions*. These convictions are *personal* because they are formed by each individual, not by a general command for the entire church. They are also personal because once these convictions are formed, they are not to be applied to others but rather practiced by oneself. They are for personal consumption, not for export. This does not mean you cannot talk to others about your convictions; it is just a reminder that the first function of our convictions is for ourselves—to express our devotion to Christ. We don't come up with our convictions to impress others or win converts. Others may be impressed by your convictions or even moved to join you in following them, but that is not their primary purpose.

Similarly, these personal convictions are *convictions* because they are not merely preferences. They are not just statements of what we happen to like or happen to think. They are convictions formed by careful reflection on what we believe Jesus happens to like or think. Our personal preferences have little to do with the matter. We know what we like—that hardly requires deliberation. Rather, we are trying to discern what is pleasing to Jesus, and knowing *his* mind requires deliberation. It should also be noted that Paul is not asking us to consider what is permissible to the Lord but rather what is pleasing to the Lord. I have discovered that we can conceive of many things as *permissible* that we would have a much harder time imagining as *pleasing* to the Lord. Paul clearly indicates in this passage that in disputable matters our goal is not to please others, nor is it to please ourselves, but rather our goal is to please Jesus. It is wise to form one's convictions by asking what is pleasing to Jesus, not simply what Jesus might permit, and certainly not just what I myself might like.

It is also possible that there may be convictions that are necessary at a particular time and place, but later or elsewhere these convictions are no longer necessary. Indeed, Paul suggests this when he talks about those who are weaker in faith. The idea is that in the course of events their faith regarding days and diets might grow and develop, and when that happens, they might change their convictions about days or diets. Furthermore, Paul wants to be sure we extend the same grace to others so that they can be fully convinced in their own minds even if their convictions are different from our own.

Principle 4: Avoid judging the strong and offending the weak. Before leaving Romans 14, we must consider specific counsel Paul gives to both the weaker and the stronger. First, concerning a person who is weaker in faith and more prone to have a hyperactive conscience, Paul knows this person is likely to see others doing things that they would refuse to do. He cautions them not to judge. If these weaker brothers and sisters fear someone is getting away with something and dishonoring Christ, Paul assures them that no one will get away with anything. Each will give an account to God (v. 12). Paul also says that in many of these matters, God seems to be able to find himself honored by people on both sides. As Paul puts it, those who eat do so in honor of the Lord; those who abstain also do so in honor of the Lord. It seems the Lord can handle diverse ways of his followers seeking to honor him.

The corresponding error of the stronger is to use their freedom in ways that offend those who are weaker: "Do not, for the sake of food, destroy the work of God. Everything is indeed clean, but it is wrong for anyone to make another stumble by what he eats. It is good not to eat meat or drink wine or do anything that causes your brother to stumble. The faith that you have, keep between yourself and God" (Rom 14:20-22 ESV).

Paul gives a simple rule of thumb: taste should give way to conviction. If it is a matter of conviction for your brother or sister, defer to their conviction instead of indulging your liberty. If you are sharing a dinner with someone who believes it is wrong to eat meat or drink wine, do not flaunt your freedom but rather defer to your brother or sister. You do not need to defer at all times—only in those times where indulging will give offense. In such cases, defer to the other person's conscience so that they are not offended.

When I (Rick) was halfway through high school, my school purchased a foosball table for the student center. Suddenly I became interested in playing foosball. I quickly learned that the game is easy to play but hard to master. The ball moves rapidly and bounces at odd angles. I got beat a lot at first, but I began to get better. Then I decided to go to a local arcade where I could play more than just during the short breaks between classes. I got better still. Unfortunately, there were still others who always beat me. I decided to work harder. After a few months of hard work, I was playing another student who always beat me. I realized halfway through the game that I could actually win. We traded goals until it came down to the final ball. I deftly passed the ball forward and hit a hard shot straight into his goal. My elation vanished when I discovered that I had hit the ball so hard it bounced right back out of his goal and rolled all the way down the table and into my goal instead. I had just hit my best shot at the perfect time, and all I did was beat myself!

I walked outside and sat on the curb in shock. After about thirty minutes of rage and frustration I heard a quiet voice saying, "Rick, you care too much about foosball." It was an irritating voice. All the more so because the message was both irritating and right. I *did* care too much about foosball. I realized that I was hearing something from Jesus and that he was telling me I needed to stop playing foosball.

At that point in my life, I needed to develop a *personal conviction* about playing foosball. It was a *personal* conviction because foosball was a problem for me personally, not everyone else. I needed to stop playing foosball, but there was no reason that my friends—whether Christian or non-Christian—should stop playing foosball. Jesus had given me a message, not them. And it was a personal *conviction* both because I was fully convinced in my own mind and also because it had nothing to do with my preferences. I still liked playing foosball; I just realized that Jesus did not like who I became when I was playing foosball. For me, giving up foosball was an important act of personal devotion.

This story illustrates the personal nature of convictions and the vital role they play in our spiritual growth. It also illustrates that sometimes a matter of mere taste for one person can be a matter of conviction for another. In other words, up until that painful game, I would have said that whether a person plays air hockey or foosball is a matter of mere taste—a personal preference. In fact, even after that day I still would have said that about my friends. But I would not have said that about myself. I could play air hockey and win or lose—it wasn't a problem. Something was different when I played foosball.

This story also illustrates how a conviction can change. Upon graduation from high school I went off to college. There was no foosball table in my dorm. Rarely did my friends play foosball. Foosball gradually became unimportant to me. A few years later, I began working with a youth group that had a foosball table. As I watched the students play, I realized my foosball obsession had passed. I was over it. I could play it like it was just a game, and so I did. And to be clear, my conviction did not change because it had been wrong; my conviction changed because it had served its purpose.

So there it is. We are to cultivate and practice personal convictions. Our convictions do not need to agree with another's, and we should avoid judging other people's convictions and also avoid "exporting" our own convictions. It should be noted that saying we should avoid judging and exporting our own convictions is different from saying we should not talk about them with others. Discussing convictions makes for well-formed convictions. Furthermore, it is certainly possible for us to be mistaken about our convictions, and discussions can help us see flaws in our thinking. Nonetheless, the first point of application for our convictions is always toward ourselves. The goal of our convictions is to guide our own conduct so that it is pleasing to Jesus, not to guide the conduct of others.

It would be nice if this were the final word. However, these guidelines for personal convictions are the start of a conversation, not the end. They leave many questions unanswered. For example, if we all agree on Scripture, how is it that we end up disagreeing about convictions? Also, how do we handle differences in convictions at an interpersonal level? Romans 14 may give us a theoretical and theological understanding of personal convictions, but what about the relational and psychological challenges of conflicting convictions? And should our disagreements about convictions force us to part ways, or should we always be able to overcome our disagreements and work together? It is questions like these we must consider in the coming chapters.

3

THE CONVICTION SPECTRUM

During the 1992 presidential election, I (Rick) was directing the small group ministry at our church. Bill Clinton was running against George H. W. Bush, and given that many evangelicals found Bill Clinton to be an unsavory political figure, a large majority of White evangelicals voted against him.

A few days after Bill Clinton was elected, I was facilitating a small-group leaders' meeting. One of the leaders whose political convictions leaned strongly Republican suggested that our small groups should have a time of lament in light of the recent election. Some others nodded in agreement.

Was this a good idea?

I thought not. There were some assumptions hidden here. First, there was a political assumption of a clear alignment between the Republican party and the Christian faith. Hence, if the Republicans lost, it would be a cause for Christians to lament. Pastor Tim Keller offers a helpful critique of this notion:

> Another reason not to align the Christian faith with one party is that most political positions are not matters of

biblical command but of practical wisdom. . . . The biblical commands to lift up the poor and to defend the rights of the oppressed are moral imperatives for believers. . . . However, there are many possible ways to help the poor. Should we shrink government and let private capital markets allocate resources, or should we expand the government and give the state more of the power to redistribute wealth? Or is the right path one of the many possibilities in between? The Bible does not give exact answers to these questions for every time, place and culture.[1]

Keller nicely states the first problem with having a season of lament. He reminds us that there is always a distance that has to be traversed between a timeless biblical command and a social policy governing affairs at a particular place and time.

A second problem seemed even more important to me. It was more pastoral than political. There is a tendency in small groups for the majority view to become the only view expressed, especially when the leader of the group shares the majority view. Proponents of the minority view often duck and cover, waiting for the conversation to move on to more congenial topics. It made me wonder how a season of lament would be perceived by certain members of our groups.

With these concerns in mind, I mentioned to the leaders that about 80 percent of evangelicals voted Republican, a fact that most seemed to be aware of. Then I asked all of the leaders to take a sheet of paper and write down the two to three people in their group who likely voted Democratic.

There was dead silence. No one picked up their pencils.

Finally, a leader spoke up and said they didn't think anyone in their group had voted Democratic. I pointed out that if our congregation reflected the national averages for evangelicals, a small group of twelve to fourteen people would have three Democrats. I was just asking them to stop and think who those people were and how they would likely feel if we opened up the small group meeting with a season of lament. It was an awkward moment. The leaders realized that opening the small group with a season of lament might not be welcomed by certain group members. They also realized that prayer times in the last several weeks leading up to the election were probably equally alienating. We had simply been blind to an underlying diversity of political convictions within our groups.

What is the solution to problems like these? Do we simply refuse to talk about politics? Should we only offer silent prayers about politics? Should Christians form political convictions based merely on their personal preferences and not try to anchor them in Scripture? Should we obey the famous saying and avoid talking about religion and politics?

We believe none of these are good solutions. Instead, we need to cultivate well-formed Christian convictions about politics and a host of other matters, and we need to be able to give an account of how these convictions emerge from our Christian faith. This is just putting Romans 14 into action.

But we need to be very thoughtful about forming our convictions. To help our thinking we will first offer a definition of convictions in general. Then we will consider some of the unique aspects of Christian convictions and how these can intensify our conflicts. Finally, we will take an in-depth look at the spectrum of conviction. Understanding this helps us make space for our brothers and sisters to have differing convictions but still be appreciated as faithful members of the body of Christ.

DEFINING CONVICTION

The standard dictionary definition of conviction runs something like this: a fixed or firmly held belief, a belief that we won't be giving up anytime soon. But we have beliefs like that about arithmetic, and we don't usually call those convictions. Convictions are not just about garden variety facts but rather about particular sorts of beliefs. We might say that convictions are *firmly held moral or religious beliefs that guide our beliefs, actions, or choices.* This shuts out beliefs we have about matters of taste (not moral), and it also shuts out beliefs we hold but are happy to disregard or ignore (they don't guide our actions). We could keep going, but this is not a philosophy book, and for our purposes, this common-sense definition should do the job.

Notice that this definition makes room for two different kinds of convictions, what we might call *absolute* convictions and *personal* convictions. Absolute convictions are called absolute not so much because of the zeal with which we hold them, but rather because we feel that they should apply to "absolutely" everyone. They are universal; they apply both to ourselves and our neighbor. The great Christian creeds are examples of such absolutes. Personal convictions, on the other hand, are things we believe personally and which guide our personal conduct, but we realize others may not share. This might be a conviction about refusing to drink alcohol because a family member had been killed by a drunk driver. We would probably hold this conviction quite firmly, but we would also know that not everyone would share it. The distinctions we are making here are nothing new; they simply reflect the famous maxim "In essentials, unity; in nonessentials, liberty; in all things, charity."

THE CHALLENGE OF CHRISTIAN CONVICTION

Next, let's make a few observations about unique aspects of Christian convictions and the challenges these pose for resolving conflicts.

First, most Christians attach their convictions to Christ personally. In other words, *we form our convictions in order to please Jesus, not ourselves.* Convictions do not express what *we* think or feel or like but rather our best understanding of what we believe *Jesus* thinks or feels or likes. Therefore, fellow believers who dispute our convictions are not saying that our convictions are displeasing to *them*; they are effectively saying that our convictions are displeasing to *Jesus.* Of course they would never put it that way, but it is natural for us to hear it that way. Christians are invested in their convictions and see them as an expression of their personal devotion to God, not merely as an expression of a personal preference.

Furthermore, Christian convictions are not just deeply personal acts of devotion, they are also grounded in absolutes. Christians usually grow their convictions in the soil of God's Word. For us, God's Word is infallible and authoritative, so conflicts would seem to arise from one of two unsavory possibilities: first, that our Christian opponent is actually not very Christian because he or she is denying the authority of God's Word. Unsavory, indeed! The other possibility is that our opponents are misrepresenting God's Word. If it is done unintentionally, these people are simply negligent. If done intentionally, it is a matter of false teaching, and one might even say they are false prophets since they offer a false belief but claim it is coming from God. Christian disputes about convictions are easily supercharged with transcendent significance. It is fine to say we should major on the majors and minor on the minors, but for Christian convictions, nothing seems to be minor!

At the emotional level, conflicting convictions are bad enough when we see or hear them at a distance. It is much worse when the conflict is with a friend or member of your small group. Christians join small groups for intimate, burden-bearing fellowship. We lay bare our souls before the Word of God that is able to pierce to the division of the joint and the marrow and before which no secret can be hidden. We also lay bare our trials and troubles—struggles with our marriages and our children, struggles with our doubts and fears and dying hopes. If a member of our small group suddenly opposes our deeply held convictions, our safe haven has become profoundly unsafe. We joined the small group for a respite from an ugly and dangerous world—it is beyond disappointing to find the ugly and dangerous sitting beside you and holding your hand during prayer time!

To summarize this with a metaphor, when a non-Christian attacks our convictions, it feels like an attack by an enemy soldier. They are dressed like the other side and they are wearing the opposing colors.

When a Christian attacks our convictions, they are standing on our side and wearing our colors. They are not an enemy solider—they are an enemy *spy!* They are a wolf in sheep's clothing.

No wonder it's difficult to deal with conflicting convictions. These observations about the way Christians form convictions are not an argument for changing the ingredients that go into our thinking. We must seek to please Jesus with our convictions since it is to him that we will give an account (Rom 14:12). Furthermore, we can and should use the Bible as a sourcebook for our convictions. After all, the Word of God is a lamp unto our feet and a light unto our path (Ps 119:105), surely it is meant to guide our beliefs, actions, and choices. And, we really are waging a spiritual war and are called to "take every thought captive to obey Christ" (2 Cor 10:5 ESV). Metaphors like crossing enemy lines are really not just figures of speech. There is no simple corrective to the special problems of Christian conviction. We are called to be people of conviction. It seems to us that there is no other choice except half-hearted devotion and cheap grace, which is really no choice at all.

THE SPECTRUM OF CONVICTION

So how can we form deep Christian convictions without dividing the church? Let's take a deeper look at convictions themselves.

Convictions are like light: they come in many colors and form across a spectrum. Consider the belief that God created human beings in his own image—a timeless theological truth grounded in Scripture (Gen 1:26). This sort of conviction could be called a *confessional belief*—an absolute that all Christians should share in common. A few chapters later, in Genesis 9:5-6, this truth is formed into a *moral mandate* which prohibits killing a person because all humans are made in the image of God. This moral mandate can be further expanded into a set of positive claims that actively *value* human life. Unpacking this a bit, we would see that valuing human life would probably mean more than just being "pro-life" in the sense of opposing abortion. Instead, one might think of a "consistent ethic of life," a phrase coined by Cardinal Joseph Bernardin.[2] Such an ethic shuns abortion but also euthanasia, war, and violence. It would likely have positive entailments such as access to basic human freedoms that image bearers require, such as the freedom to worship according to one's conscience and have basic necessities such as food and shelter. These increasingly refined judgments do not emerge because we are finding more and more explicit teachings of Scripture, but because we are unpacking more and more implications of our confessional belief that human beings are created in the image of God. These implications might be summarized in a core value statement such as, "Every human being should be protected from life-threatening harms and provided access to essential goods needed for a flourishing human life."

Clearly we are moving across a spectrum and becoming increasingly specific as we go. Our confessional beliefs and moral mandates are shaping *core values* within our souls—shaping our desires and pursuits. However, these core values are still not specific enough. Ultimately, we must discern specific *guidelines for conduct*. We must decide if the prohibition against taking the life of an image bearer means that we should oppose both abortion and capital punishment or only abortion. Does a pro-life commitment mean we should favor pacifism rather than a just war? We must decide if access to basic human goods includes only food and shelter or if it also includes access to basic health care. And if it does include access to health care, does that mean we should advocate for universal health care, or are there better ways to meet this basic human need?

Figure 3.1 summarizes this movement across the spectrum of conviction.

Notice that as we move across this spectrum each step makes our convictions more specific, but as they become more specific, they also become more contested. At the outset, explicit statements of Scripture or universal creedal confessions assure agreement among all Christians. Convictions about these matters are absolute and universal. However, the more specific we make our judgments, the

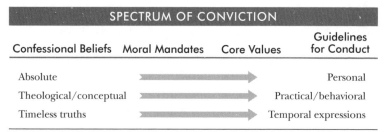

Figure 3.1. Movement across the spectrum of conviction

more culture, prudence, historical circumstance, and practical wisdom influence our conclusions, and therefore the more diverse our opinions become.

We can connect this spectrum to the three different types of issues mentioned in the previous chapter: absolutes, disputable matters which are included in this spectrum, and matters of taste which are not. The spectrum begins on the left with absolutes and moves right as it increasingly addresses disputable matters. At the far right would be matters of taste, but they are not included because they are not matters about which we form convictions.

Confessional beliefs. Confessional beliefs define the boundaries of Christianity and ground the beliefs and practices of the church and individual believers. They are often expressed in creedal statements such as the Apostles' Creed or the Nicene Creed. Creedal statements are commonly recited by the whole church in public worship. They are also generally worded as "We believe" statements rather than "I believe" statements. Clearly the implication is that all members of the congregation are expected to share these beliefs. Denying these creedal statements is good grounds for doubting the authenticity of a person's Christian faith. These confessional beliefs serve as preconditions for our convictions. We might even call them Christian convictions as opposed to personal convictions exactly because we believe that these convictions are part and parcel of the Christian faith itself. They are not simply matters of personal conviction.

As the name implies, confessional beliefs focus on *belief* not action. They are largely composed of timeless theological assertions about the nature of God, mankind, and salvation. Since creedal statements are intentionally timeless, they lack specificity relative to questions that arise within particular societies and cultures. Saying "Jesus is Lord" clearly has entailments for action—but those entailments are not made explicit by the phrase itself. Churches and individual disciples of Christ have to decide what honoring Jesus as Lord demands of them in the particular times and cultural circumstances in which they find themselves.

Moral mandates. Identifying moral and spiritual mandates is the first step in "operationalizing" our confessional beliefs—that is, moving them into action. Like confessional beliefs, moral and spiritual mandates are universal or near universal among Christians. They are the behavioral counterparts to the theological beliefs found in our confessional statements and creeds and are derived from the commands of Scripture, even as the confessional beliefs are derived from the theological claims of Scripture.

"Mandates" is a handy way to refer to these high-level action-guiding principles, but it should be noted that the term covers a wide range of behaviors. Some of these mandates address *spiritual* issues related to proper worship and devotion to God. Other commands deal with *ethical* issues about how we treat fellow human beings. In what follows we will use the phrase "moral mandates" as an umbrella term that covers both ethical and spiritual matters. We hope that "moral" nicely captures the sense of obligation that mandates have, but it should be understood broadly enough to include the mandates of Scripture regarding both ethical conduct and spiritual devotion.

A good example of a moral mandate is the summary of the law given by Jesus himself: "'Love the Lord your God with all your heart and with all your soul and with all your strength and with all your mind'; and, 'Love your neighbor as yourself'" (Lk 10:27). This short statement summarizes the vastly more complex set of commandments found in the Old Testament. Hidden in this statement is a transition from confessional belief to a behavioral command—from confessional beliefs to moral mandates. The passage begins by confessing: "Hear, O Israel: the LORD our God, the LORD is one" (Deut 6:4). It then proceeds to a pair of behavioral mandates—one spiritual and one moral: to love the Lord our God with all that we are and all that we have (spiritual), and to love our neighbor as ourselves (moral).

Moral mandates, as we use the term here, tend to be few in number and broad in application. There is no exact definition of the phrase "few in number and broad in application." Jesus offers a twofold command in the example above. But one might also view the Ten Commandments as a set of moral mandates. Indeed, the Ten Commandments directly unpack the two great commandments in the sense that they are divided into two "tablets": the first, which pertains to loving God, and the second, which pertains to loving human beings. We already see here a spectrum forming that moves from small numbers of broad commands to larger numbers of increasingly narrow commands.

In addition to the commands and teachings of Scripture, one may also find mandates in other places. Consider the statement from the Westminster Confession that the chief end of man is to love God and enjoy him forever. This statement once again moves us from what we believe to what we are to do. It also applies to a very broad range of activities in and through which we can love and enjoy God.

Core values. Moral and spiritual mandates almost immediately beg for further specification. For example, if the chief end of man is to love God and enjoy him forever, what must I do to honor this mandate? Does enjoying God mean worshiping in song and partaking of the sacraments, or does it include enjoying his creation? Does this statement require me to attend church on a Sunday morning, or does it permit me to sit by a mountain stream? Does it mean that I should have a daily quiet time, or are other spiritual disciplines more important? Moral mandates are like the North Star: they help you know what direction to go but don't provide a step-by-step map or even instructions as to whether you should travel by ship, land, or air.

The next step, then, is to identify values and commitments that offer more specific guidance for our moral mandates and confessional beliefs. We have labeled this next step along our conviction spectrum "core values," referring to the things that are important to us—the things that we actually value. The term "values" is commonly used by moral psychologists or sociologists to identify underlying motivations for actions. Values are desired ends that guide us in our choices and help us evaluate policies, people, and events. Recently, social psychologist Jonathan Haidt has formulated a "Moral Foundations Theory" that identifies six basic human values: care, fairness, loyalty, authority, sanctity, and liberty.[3] His work builds on pioneering work done by others, including Shalom Schwartz, who spent four decades researching dozens of cultures and ultimately identifying a set of ten universal human values.[4] For our present purposes, the number and exact definition of these values is not important. What is important is that both Haidt and Schwartz identified a set of core values that they believe all people shared despite the radical differences between cultures.

How can common values result in such different guidelines for action? The reason is that people tend to agree about the values themselves but tend to disagree on how the values should be *prioritized*. Most controversial issues intersect more than one value, as in the case where a policy that promotes liberty may diminish fairness or fail to care for a basic human need. Different groups of people may agree on values and even upon which values apply but disagree on how heavily to weigh each value. For example, when discussing immigration, everyone may agree that people should obey governing authorities and also regard immigrants with love and dignity, but they may disagree on how to weigh these in particular cases. Furthermore, people do not construct a single, universal hierarchy of value but rather may prioritize values differently depending on the situation. In other words, we might weigh values differently in the case of Syrian refugees and Central Americans crossing our southern border. In short, *values are the place a common starting point leads to different end points.*

In addition to that which all human beings might value, Christians will hold certain unique values because of their shared faith. For example, we value personal devotion to God. Christians generally find it important to engage in practices that build intimacy with God—practices like Bible study, prayer, and spiritual disciplines. We might also identify the value of obedience and submission, both obeying commands but also discerning and submitting to God's providential ordering of our lives—being willing to go where he leads us (even if we do not want to go). There is also the value of caring for the marginalized and oppressed, particularly offering charity toward the sick, strangers, and prisoners as is mentioned in Matthew 25. We value the cultivation of virtue and personal holiness; we value right belief and faithful worship; we value refusing to be conformed to this world and having a willingness to be a "peculiar people . . . zealous of good works" (Titus 2:14 GNV). Presumably all or almost all Christians would value all of these things. However, how highly we value them would vary from Christian to Christian. For example, most evangelical Christians value evangelism, which is hardly surprising—it's in the name! Most other groups of Christians value outreach as well, although outreach activities may vary from group to group. These differences in values, and the valuing of our values, go a long way toward explaining the diversity of our convictions.

Values are also deeply internalized and emotionally charged. We assent to belief and obey commands, but we *feel* our values. Well-formed convictions involve the total person—intellect, will, and emotion. An unfelt conviction is really no conviction at all—it is not yet fully formed in us if we do not feel it internally, and it is largely at the point of values that our feelings begin to emerge.

An illustration of the move from moral mandates to core values is found in the Gospel of Luke. Jesus has just identified the two great commandments, to love God and to love one's neighbor.

These are what we have labeled "moral mandates." The audience immediately wants further specification. They ask, "Who is my neighbor?" Jesus realizes that something more than just an abstract definition is needed. So he offers one of his most emotionally moving parables, the parable of the good Samaritan. He is telling a story to help his hearers understand what neighbor love really looks like and especially how it really *feels*—both to receive neighbor love and to refuse to offer it. His point is that neighbor love leaps across boundaries of ethnicity and prejudice in its zeal to help a person in need. He is commending a passionate care, not a detached principle. Boundary crossing love is a Christian value.

Almost two thousand years after Jesus offered this parable, Martin Neimöller, a leader of the Confessing Church that opposed the Nazi regime, offered a statement that performs a similar task. Both Jesus' parable and Niemöller's words contextualize neighbor love into the contexts of their respective days while giving a sense of the emotions that should properly attach to it:

> First they came for the Socialists, and I did not speak out—
> Because I was not a Socialist.
> Then they came for the Trade Unionists, and I did not speak out—
> Because I was not a Trade Unionist.
> Then they came for the Jews, and I did not speak out—
> Because I was not a Jew.
> Then they came for me—and there was no one left to speak for me.[5]

Neimöller is placing the moral mandate of neighbor love within his immediate social context—a context that included socialists, trade unionists, and Jews, rather than Samaritans. He also creates a haunting, visceral sense of the tragedy of refusing neighbor love that is quite similar to the feelings evoked in Jesus' parable as the Levite and the priest walk by on the other side of the road from where the Samaritan lay hurt and helpless.

Guidelines for conduct. The final step along the conviction spectrum is developing specific guidelines for conduct. Here, moral mandates and core values find expression in actual policy decisions, responses to ethical dilemmas, and plans for action within a specific cultural context. Guidelines for conduct have time frames, locations, and audiences in mind. They answer the question, How can I best honor Christ in the time and place and circumstance where he has placed me?

The importance of practical wisdom. Practical wisdom and knowledge play an extremely important role in forming guidelines for conduct. As quoted earlier, Tim Keller argues that caring for the poor is a clear biblical teaching and a moral mandate, but it is a matter of practical wisdom as to whether the best way to do this is through private enterprise or government redistribution or some combination of the two. Similarly, neighbor love and the protection of life in the image of God mandates that we alleviate human suffering and care for the afflicted. Moral mandates to this effect are found throughout Scripture. But does this include providing basic health care? Well, it seemed to in the parable of the good Samaritan, but what does that mean today? Do we need to provide universal health care? If so, do we do this through the Affordable Care Act, private insurance, or a single-payer health care system? The answers to questions like these will be found by studying the economics involved, the effectiveness of the health care delivered, and the actual access people have to that care. These are not exegetical questions but questions of practice. There is no single "Christian" answer to questions like these. Nonetheless, we must decide what we will do. We cannot pursue all options at once. We have to land our plane and not just circle the airport.

The importance of guidelines of conduct. As one moves across the spectrum from absolutes to personal convictions, it is easy to think that one is moving from the more important to less important, but this is misleading for several reasons:

1. The conviction spectrum moves from defining beliefs universally held by all Christians to personal convictions practiced by particular disciples. It is a movement from the *definition* of the faith to the *expression* of the faith, a movement from beliefs to actions. A well-formed Christian faith simply requires both. Furthermore, when it comes to being salt and light to a watching world, what is often most important is specific actions—the good works marked out by our guidelines for conduct.

2. Guidelines of conduct are not only important for our public witness but are also extremely important for personal growth and devotion. I (Rick) remember a couple who experienced a terrible moral failure and had been removed from Christian leadership because of a sexual addiction. This led the couple to get involved in a twelve-step group, and this involvement transformed their lives in a radical way. In fact, they would say that working a Christian twelve-step program was really the point at which their Christian faith became a reality in their lives. The twelve steps gave tangible expression to many of the confessional beliefs and moral mandates that they previously had only been nominally committed to—mandates and beliefs like our complete dependence upon Christ, our inability to save ourselves, and the necessity of repentance and restitution. Without specific guidelines of conduct, these beliefs and mandates had remained largely intellectual and unexpressed. When the couple began to work a twelve-step program they adopted a set of guidelines for conduct that operationalized these previously dormant confessional beliefs and moral mandates.

3. In short, specific guidelines of conduct are extremely important. Guidelines for conduct help us show our faith by our works, to borrow the language that James uses. They enable us to fulfill Paul's exhortation to be "a peculiar people . . . zealous of good works" (Titus 2:14 GNV). None of this

should ever imply that works are more important than faith—but simply that fully formed faith demands expression in tangible works done within the circumstances in which God has providentially placed us. These works may look different for different believers at different times and places. What is really important is not to rank our confessional beliefs as more important than our guidelines for conduct, or vice versa, but rather to work our confessional beliefs all the way out to specific guidelines of conduct. Anything short of that leads to a nominal faith and a muted witness to the watching world.

BACK TO THE SMALL GROUP

Let's conclude by returning to the question of how a small group Bible study should respond to an election. Joining together for a season of lament assumes an agreement on political convictions that is probably not a reality. Our goal in a situation like this is that a diversity of political convictions should be both expected and respected.

Respecting differing convictions does not mean we do nothing because there are differences between our group members. If possible, group members should be given an opportunity to express not only their viewpoints but also some of the reasons behind them. The goal is to refine and deepen one another's convictions. If the argument of this chapter is true, we will answer to Jesus for our political convictions. They need to be well-formed and well-attached to confessional beliefs that all Christians hold in common. Talking about our convictions and even asking questions of others is not forbidden, but our hope is that our interactions with one another will lead to better-formed personal convictions for each individual. The goal is not to produce a single accepted conviction for the entire group.

Here are some ways a small group might refine one another's thinking. The suggestions are arranged in the order of increasing amounts of time and effort required.

- Open a prayer time by having each member of the group share a prayer request for our country in light of the recent election. This is simple and requires very little time but does offer a chance for group members to respond differently to the election. The leader would probably want to say at the outset that different members of the group are likely to feel differently about the election.

- If more time is available, have people share prayer requests about some issue facing our country, and also give each person a few minutes to explain why that issue is particularly important to him or her. Often our personal life experience shapes our judgments about the practical wisdom of social policies. Sharing our stories can foster much deeper understanding and appreciation of conflicting viewpoints.

- Have the small group read and respond to the quote at the beginning of this chapter from Tim Keller. Then as a group identify some confessional beliefs and moral and spiritual mandates that might undergird Christian thinking on political matters. Seek to identify beliefs and mandates that would be affirmed by all. Keller's examples are the rejection of racism based on the command to love our neighbor as ourselves. He also mentions the priority of caring for the poor and disenfranchised, which is also based on explicit biblical teaching. Keller's examples are just a start; many other examples could be given. Once the group has identified some of these shared confessional beliefs or moral mandates, individuals could share how they attach their contemporary political convictions to these higher-level commitments.

We often underestimate the peer pressure of a small group. It is important that a group help each member articulate his or her viewpoints. We should be particularly careful to hear from minority viewpoints within our small groups, and we should also be careful to protect and support those who hold these viewpoints, extending grace to all and not assuming everyone has thoroughly thought through their convictions. Such grace is particularly needed for those who hold minority views. When you hold the majority viewpoint, no one will disparage you if you offer an inadequate expression of the viewpoint—instead they will chime in and prop up your comments. If you hold the minority view, however, it is much less natural for people to be gracious and supportive, especially if this view is inadequately expressed. Leaders need to be particularly sensitive to being supportive in such situations.

In general, it is not uncommon for us to have strong, gut-level intuitions about moral and political issues. This is not necessarily wrong—our conscience often operates intuitively without our being able to identify principles that would support our intuition. However, it is valuable to refine and deepen our intuitions by reasoned reflection illuminated by the wisdom of others. We are not the self-sufficient source of all truth. Jennifer Herdt, a Christian ethicist at Yale Divinity School, notes that a deep dependence on God is essential to developing "truthfulness concerning one's own character and capacities [which] enables the admission of weakness and strength, incapacity and capacity, alike."[6] She goes on to point out that virtues like courtesy and forbearance "guard against the illusion of self-sufficiency [and] are needed in order to sustain the kind of communal relationship within which the common good can be pursued."[7] We pursue truth together, as part of a community. An essential part of this process is, as James says, being "open to reason, full of mercy and good fruits, impartial and sincere." Such virtues lead to a "harvest of righteousness" (Jas 3:17-18 ESV). Once we have listened to others with openness and sincerity, we are in a much better place to pursue Paul's project of becoming "fully convinced in [our] own mind" (Rom 14:5).

SECTION II

COMMUNICATING
CONVICTIONS

4

DOES DIVISION HAVE TO BE DIVISIVE?

To this point, we have been answering two questions: How should we cultivate personal convictions, and how should we live together when they differ? The key to answering both of these questions is understanding that we use the word *convictions* to cover a spectrum ranging from confessional beliefs that define the faith to guidelines for conduct that help us express the faith in tangible deeds. We should expect agreement at the level of confessional beliefs, but we should not expect universal agreement when it comes to guidelines for conduct. Indeed, Romans 14 assumes that believers will express their commitment to Christ by following various guidelines for conduct and that we should respect each other's freedom to do this. This does not mean that we lack convictions or simply respond to differing convictions by saying, "Whatever." Rather, we have deep convictions that are thoughtfully developed and prayerfully refined. Other members of the body of Christ do not need to agree with our personal convictions, but they should respect them even as we respect theirs.

So far, so good.

However, a looming question remains unaddressed. Our discussion of Romans 14 associated personal convictions with "disputable matters" but acknowledged that some things are *not* disputable matters. Some things are absolutes that all Christians should agree upon. What happens when we disagree about absolutes? Is division permissible? And what about dividing fellowship when one group thinks an issue is an absolute and another group does not? And even with disputable matters, are these disputes ever of such a nature that we could or should divide fellowship?

These are difficult questions. This chapter will argue that there are times when it is permissible and prudent for Christians to divide fellowship, not only in disagreements about absolutes but also in the case of certain disputable matters. In most cases Christian unity demands that we live together with our differing convictions, but there are times when the best way to preserve Christian unity is by parting ways.

UNITY AND DIVISION

Division because of false teaching. To begin with the most obvious cases, consider false teachers who deny the confessional beliefs that define Christianity. Should we disfellowship a false teacher or divide a church in which some members are committed to following a false teacher?

In the New Testament the answer appears to be "Yes!" Truth is important. Merely believing a proposition does not guarantee the proposition is true. Our reasoning is often flawed and always imperfect, and it is easy for us to have false beliefs. Perhaps even more significant is that the truth of our beliefs *matter*. Truth leads to life; falsehood leads to death. Jesus is the way and the truth and the life while Satan is the father of lies, and following his lies leads us on the path of destruction.

These simple facts go a long way to explaining the harsh words one finds in the New Testament for false teaching. False teachers are not just a cognitive problem because they spread false beliefs, they are a peril to our very souls. False teaching confounds our minds with error even as it corrupts our souls with polluted desires and misplaced affections. For this reason, the New Testament saves some of its strongest language for condemning false teachers. Jesus likens false teachers to ravenous wolves dressed up like innocent sheep and cautions his followers to beware (Mt 7:15). He warns that the end times will be marked by an increase in false teaching and strongly warns against being deceived and led astray (Mt 24:11, 24). Paul offers similar condemnations, identifying false teachers by name (1 Tim 1:20; 2 Tim 4:14) and calling them out for punishment. In 2 Peter 2, Peter offers lengthy, specific, and emphatic condemnations of false teaching. He notes that false prophets expound false doctrinal beliefs, even denying Jesus himself (v. 1) but they also follow their own sensuality or greed and thereby bring shame upon the "way of truth" (v. 2). Later in the chapter, they are said to indulge in the lust of defiling passions and despise authority (v. 10). Their passions lead them both into sexual immorality and into greed and gain from wrongdoing (vv. 14-15). False teachers promise freedom but offer only bondage and destruction (v. 19). John also condemns false teachers in strong language. He sees false teaching manifest by moral failure—people who profess to know Christ but fail to keep his commandments (1 Jn 2:4-6). He is also concerned with doctrinal failure—people denying the humanity of Christ (1 Jn 4:2; 2 Jn 7) and the deity of Christ (1 Jn 2:22-23). Finally, he shares Peter's concern of a false teacher rejecting authority (3 Jn 9).

The particular doctrinal errors of false teachers in the New Testament vary, but they are always profound and fundamental. Some false teachers deny the resurrection, and some deny the incarnation. The denial of these historical aspects of the faith lead to corresponding denials of either the deity or the humanity of Christ. Some false teachers argue that sins of the body don't matter, while other false teachers are greedy for financial gain. In certain cases, a specific heretical belief is not noted but a general tendency to stir up controversy and dissension is (Titus 3:9-11). In general, false teachers reject other authorities and operate as authorities unto themselves.

The gravity of these errors is such that separation or limitation of fellowship is either mandated, implied, or permitted in the hope that even worse final judgment might be averted. False teachers are to be warned once or twice and then we are to have nothing more to do with them (Titus 3:9-11). Paul wants them handed over to Satan that they may learn not to blaspheme (1 Tim 1:20). He refers to other false teachers as dogs and evildoers (Phil 3:2) and as people whose god is their bellies, who glory in their shame (Phil 3:19). These are people who are to be marked and avoided, even as those who follow Paul's teaching are to be noted and followed as good examples (Phil 3:17). Peter states that the gloom of utter darkness has been reserved for them (2 Pet 2:17) and strongly cautions his hearers to avoid these teachers (2 Pet 2:19-21; 3:17). John identifies these teachers for his readers so that they will not extend hospitality to them (2 Jn 10-11).

In summary, the New Testament makes clear that: (1) there are false teachers who try to make their way into faithful Christian fellowships, (2) false teaching corrupts both mind and body and leads to conduct that brings shame upon the church, and (3) the church should distance herself from these teachers either by avoiding them if they are outside the church or by removing them from fellowship if they are within the church. Clearly in these cases, there is a place for division. Indeed, false teaching is divisive, and for that reason the New Testament calls for a quick and clean separation. The goal is not to maintain relations with the false teacher but rather to create a clear enough divide that the shameful behavior or blasphemous claims of these false teachers cannot possibly be attributed to the faithful bride of Christ. The hope is that false teachers and their followers will be separated from the body of Christ and experience a profound loss that in turn produces repentance and opens the door for restoration.

The New Testament teaching on false prophets may seem severe and outdated in our contemporary world. I know I (Rick) thought this way—until I didn't.

My wake-up call came in my early twenties. Upon graduation from college I joined a yearlong overseas mission project which involved intensive door-to-door evangelism and a variety of other outreaches. It was spiritually challenging, something like a Christian boot camp. Several months into our time, a speaker from the United States came to lead a spiritual renewal retreat. He was an unusually charismatic speaker. He was confrontational, challenging, and motivational. We were encouraged to go deeper and be more radical in our faith. He would quote lengthy portions of the Bible from memory and draw fascinating and important insights from them. He was always making us see things that we had never seen before. He would usually refuse to give the actual biblical reference— challenging us to read the Bible and find it on our own.

Sometimes his theology seemed startling to me—but so much of what he said was intended to awaken us from our spiritual slumber that I figured my theology could use a little startling. He didn't deny the deity of Christ or use Scripture other than the Bible. One thing I remember in particular was a comment he made about sin. He said sin wasn't about the body; it was about the spirit. It doesn't matter what you do with your body, he said; the body is just physical matter. What really counts is your spirit, because sin is always and only a spiritual issue.

His impact on our project was transformative in every way. Most all of us felt awakened in some sense. All of us felt challenged. Upon completing our overseas stay, many of the participants in our mission project came back to the United States, and some found their way to the church where this charismatic preacher served as pastor. It made sense—where else could they find teaching and insights like what he offered? Other Bible teachers seemed mundane by comparison.

Then one day I got a phone call. This preacher had sexually violated almost two dozen of the women involved in our project—some during the original visit and others in the three years since we had come back. I was stunned; everyone was stunned. I remember gathering together with these friends, hearing tearful and tragic stories. I remember praying for healing, praying for hope, and hoping against hope that other friends who were still involved in the group would be persuaded to get out.

These events left a lifelong impression on me. I have never since doubted the importance of doctrinal truth. I have never since thought that false prophets are only in the past. I have thought back to his teaching that sharply divided the spiritual and the material world and made sin a matter of the spirit only. In many ways, this modern-day preacher was simply repackaging a particular version of the ancient heresy of Gnosticism. As the *Zondervan Encyclopedia of the Bible* describes it, "Some Gnostic leaders are high-minded ascetics, and others are licentious charlatans. Nevertheless, they all offer knowledge—and in a form or degree not to be found outside their own teaching."[1] My friends and I had encountered a licentious charlatan who eagerly offered knowledge in a form and degree not found outside his own teaching. The destruction he left in his wake still appalls me decades later.

And there are many other false teachings today. There are groups like the Jehovah's Witnesses and the Church of Jesus Christ of Latter-day Saints that deny the deity of Christ—a modern revival of the Arian heresy (lest one think that only Gnostics have made a comeback). Various groups deny the Trinity. Some leaders in several Christian denominations deny the reality of the resurrection. The many versions of what is called the prosperity gospel range from poor exegesis to full-blown heresy. Heresies were destructive in New Testament times, and they are still destructive today. For as much as this book is a plea for respectful understanding of those with differing convictions, it is not a plea for denying the possibility of real and intractable conflicts that are born of a fundamental opposition to the essential truths of the Christian faith. We still need to test every teaching and choose to hold fast only to that which is good.

It is clear the Bible teaches that there are departures from sound belief and practice that justify division. Sometimes division is simply separating a particular false teacher from the rest of the church. Sometimes a church as a whole may embrace a false teaching and needs to be separated from a denomination. Sometimes groups of churches have intractable disagreements about doctrinal issues and new denominations form as a result. Hopefully, these all concern issues where at least one group (if not both) believe that a confessional belief or moral mandate of the Christian faith was at stake. But are there other times when we can divide for lesser issues? We believe the answer is yes.

Separation for missional differences. The most notable example of a separation that does not appear to have anything to do with false doctrine is the argument between Paul and Barnabas described in Acts 15, verses 36-41. Ironically, they had just worked through the first church council, resolving the divisive doctrinal issue of whether or not Gentiles would be required to keep the Jewish Law. They had been promulgating the decision of the Jerusalem Council and then turned their attention to another missionary trip to strengthen the churches they had recently planted. Barnabas wanted to bring along John Mark, Paul did not since he had abandoned them in the midst of a previous mission trip. There is no heresy noted; neither is there any hint of immorality. One might call this a missional dispute rather than a doctrinal dispute, but it was clearly a dispute! In fact, it became so sharp that Paul and Barnabas decided to part ways, Barnabas taking John Mark and sailing for Cyprus, Paul taking Silas and going to Syria and Cilicia.

It is notable that in this case, there is no call from Paul for others to have nothing to do with Barnabas or vice versa. This is more of a separation of ways than a division of the body of Christ. Indeed, as events unfold there are other mentions of Barnabas by Paul, and always in a positive light. Furthermore, John Mark is mentioned later on and is commended as a person the church should welcome (Col 4:10). Later still, Paul asks for John Mark to be brought to him because he is so useful to him in carrying out his ministry (2 Tim 4:11).

I. Howard Marshall offers a helpful summary of this dispute:

Paul . . . was concerned for the mission and was unwilling to take a doubtful partner. It is a classic example of the perpetual problem of whether to place the interests of the individual or of the work as a whole first, and there is no rule of thumb for dealing with it. In this particular case a happy solution was reached in that Paul was able to choose his own companion for his part of the work, while Barnabas was able to take Mark under his wing and help him to develop as a missionary. That Barnabas's step was justified is shown by the way in which Paul later acknowledged the worth of Mark and regarded him as a colleague (Col. 4:10; and especially 2 Tim. 4:11; cf. 1 Pet. 5:12).[2]

It would seem then, that despite the contentious argument, the outcome was actually one that served the mission of the church rather well. Barnabas helped restore a minister of the gospel and was so successful that John Mark ended up winning Paul over and becoming useful to Paul once again. At the same time, the needs of the new churches of the Mediterranean world were served by Paul and Silas.

In the conviction spectrum, this would be an example of differing values—in this case values relating to missional issues. Both parties to the dispute are faithful to the gospel, teaching sound doctrine and honoring Christ in their personal lives and conduct. However, their vision for their ministries point in two different directions, and upon consideration (and a certain amount of argument) it became clear that these different visions could not be carried out effectively by all parties traveling and working together.

But notice that this missional dispute did not lead to a division in the body of Christ. It did not lead to people speaking ill of one another. It did not lead to the participants falling out of communication with one another—or at least if so, that communication was quickly restored. Unlike the case of false teachers, the separation was not intended to delineate the faithful who were bringing glory to Christ from the unfaithful who were dishonoring him. Instead, Paul and Barnabas separated in order to pursue complementary ministries that would each enhance the gospel and glorify Christ. Once the disagreement was put behind them, they spoke well of one another, continued to communicate with one another, and were able to work with one another at a later time when circumstances were different. In light of this, it is clear that all separations are not created equal and that in some cases, it may very well be possible that separating coworkers for the sake of carrying out complementary missions is actually the best way forward.

Avoiding unnecessary separation. We have just argued that separation can be biblically warranted not only in the case of heresy and blatant immorality but also in cases where missional visions diverge. Nonetheless, the circumstances that justify such separations are extremely rare. Ordinarily, the goal is that we agree in the Lord and continue to work together. This is clearly the vision of Romans 14, but it also emerges in many other contexts.

For example, Philippians identifies false teachers who are dividing the body—in this case the circumcision party. Paul wants to distance himself and the church from this destructive legalistic heresy that diminishes the work of Christ, creates false obstacles to salvation, and fosters needless division between Jews and Gentiles. On the other hand, Paul also notes people who are preaching the gospel from envy and rivalry. These false motives disturb Paul, and he wonders aloud if these people are seeking to afflict him further in the midst of his imprisonments. Does he want to see these people disfellowshiped? No! He simply says that in all cases Christ is preached and in that he rejoices. Again, it appears that there is no doctrinal heresy—all parties are preaching Christ. Therefore, he chooses to concentrate on unity and rejoice in the good that comes and leave the problematic motives to be sorted out by the Holy Spirit.

Later in Philippians, Euodia and Syntyche are engaged in a disagreement of such a magnitude that it comes to Paul's attention as he is in prison. He does not encourage them to be disfellowshiped for divisiveness, nor does he encourage them to peacefully part ways. Rather, he entreats the church to rally around them, help them reconcile, exactly so that they can return to laboring together. Clearly the normal preference and expectation of the New Testament is that disagreements should be reconciled and ministry should be carried forward together, worship should be harmonious, and all believers should preserve the unity of the Spirit and maintain the bond of peace.

DIVISIONS AND FENCES

Let's summarize what we have said thus far. Two important truths emerge from our consideration of New Testament teaching: (1) separation is permissible and at times is necessary, and (2) when separation is called for, one should choose the least disruptive options. When false teachers lead church members into a destructive heresy, they are to be disfellowshiped. Excommunication is about as disruptive as it gets. But other times, only a minimal intervention is required. Certain people may be doing things that evoke envy and rivalry. In this case a rebuke is called for, but no real separation is needed. And other cases are not matters of wrongs at all—neither wrongs big nor small. Paul and Barnabas just had different missional visions. They could simply part ways in what one might call a "mere separation."

It is helpful to do some creative thinking about options for separation that fall short of complete division. Complete division may be needed to preserve the essentials of the Christian faith and protect it from false teachers. In such cases, successful division is measured by the absence of ongoing relationship. The desire is that people both inside and outside of the church would see the divided groups as fundamentally different. But divisions are severely disruptive, so it is good to consider other alternatives first. For example, instead of dividing, one might consider building a fence. If you build a fence, you build because you want to *keep the relationship intact.* Indeed, the idea behind the saying "good fences make good neighbors" is that building a fence helps to keep your neighbor your neighbor! It keeps his dog in his backyard and your kid's baseball in your backyard. It assures that the dog won't eat the baseball and that the baseball won't break the window. And that in turn opens the door to enjoying a neighborhood picnic in either backyard!

What would the fence-building option look like in real life? In my years as a pastor, I (Rick) knew several churches that chose to do a church plant instead of a church split. Some members were at odds about important issues but not issues of confessional beliefs that define the Christian faith. Though they realized they could not live together for the long term, they could still work together in the short term, so they decided to plant another church while relationships were still intact. The church members could part peacefully and with each other's blessing. I would point out that this option works best when people realize it is an option early on. The longer a church waits, the stronger factions grow, and the stronger the factions the more likely a church will split instead of plant.

Another fence-making option I have seen be effective deals with the "sign gifts" like speaking in tongues and healing. Some churches forbid the practice of these gifts because they believe that they were only for the apostolic age; other churches believe these gifts are a necessary sign of the filling of the Holy Spirit. It is very difficult for these two positions to coexist in the same church. However, in many congregations people acknowledge that the nature and practice of the sign gifts is a "disputable matter" and a sort of fence can be erected. Usually the fences consist of policies or clear expectations about appropriate and inappropriate contexts for exercising these gifts. Usually this means specifying appropriate contexts: private use, small group use, or use in public worship services. It may also include guidelines for interpersonal communication that discourages members of the church from trying to convert other people to their side. Yes, it is a fence and it requires regular maintenance, but if well-tended, it can serve a congregation remarkably well. Tensions remain, but I have worked with both churches and Christian organizations that have flourished for decades with arrangements like this.

In short, try to limit divisions to times and places where it is absolutely necessary. In some cases merely letting people pursue different missional priorities will resolve the tensions. In other cases, we may need to exhort everyone to take a deep breath and just live together. In still other cases, exploration of creative fence-building options may give everyone enough freedom to follow Christ as they see fit while at the same time identifying clear enough boundaries to keep toes from being stepped on.

TIPS FOR NECESSARY SEPARATIONS

Here are a few tips to keep in mind when you realize that separation (in one form or another) is inevitable:

Make the reasons for the separation explicit. Explicit is actually a word that could stand being made more explicit. In the case of false teaching, an explicit statement should be one that the false teacher would look at and affirm as his own position but the faithful advocate of the gospel would reject. Likewise, the false teacher needs to be able to articulate orthodoxy in a manner that the orthodox would affirm. Until we can state each other's opinions in a manner recognizable to our opponents, we have not actually discovered if we have a real conflict or simply a misunderstanding. A misunderstanding may involve a disagreement, but it might also be nothing more than poor communication about an issue the parties actually agree upon.

It is not always easy to sort out questions like this. The two most important affirmations of the Protestant Reformation are summarized in the phrases *sola Scriptura* and *sola fide*—Latin phrases that mean "Scripture alone" and "faith alone." The phrases have a long history as ways to summarize Luther's bone of contention with the Catholic Church, namely that the Catholic Church *added works to faith* as a condition of salvation and also made the councils of the

Church equal to the Scriptures as *sources of ultimate authority* for Christian faith and practice. During the Reformation, these statements appeared to state intractable disagreements to both parties. But in recent years, some leaders of both Catholics and Protestants have been seeking to clarify the actual points of contention. Does a Catholic view the sacraments as works that are added to faith, or do they view them as means of grace that nourish saving faith? Does a Catholic view the popes and councils as authoritative in their own right and independently of Scripture, or are they authoritative interpreters of the Scriptures? Various task forces and working groups have been addressing these questions, including many people who are very conservative in their doctrinal positions (particularly the ecumenical document *Evangelicals and Catholics Together*). Their statements have not led to reunification between the branches of Christianity, but they have been helpful in clarifying what is actually meant by the central doctrinal affirmations of each group. In some cases this may diminish the distance between the groups, but even if it does not, it is helpful to make the point of disagreement explicit and thereby help all parties understand what is really at stake.

Avoid saying the grass is browner on the other side of the fence. The famous saying is that the grass is always greener on the other side, but in the case of separations between coworkers, the opposite is often true. One looks across the fence of separation and all one can see is the other ministry's failings and shortcomings. The grass seems to look *browner* on the other side.

Paul and Barnabas avoid this pitfall. They model good fences because they could see and appreciate the green in each other's grass after the fence of separation had been built. It seems clear that both continued to serve God, to serve the church, and ultimately to serve each other. At the very least the fuller record we have of Paul demonstrates all three of these outcomes. At the point of departure, they both go off to serve the church—the only difference is where and with whom. Furthermore, it seems Paul had every confidence in Barnabas himself as a faithful servant of God; he was simply concerned about the faithfulness of John Mark. Paul later mentions Barnabas directly in 1 Corinthians 9:6, comparing him to both Peter and Paul as servants of the church who have every right to earn their living from their ministry.

And not only did Paul perceive Barnabas as serving God and the church, he was also able to see Barnabas offering a service to Paul himself. The result was the restoration of John Mark, who is referred to several times in Paul's later epistles as a person who is a valuable fellow worker and who is very useful and very much a comfort to Paul in this time of need.

Indeed, one would be hard pressed to find a fence that made better neighbors than the one that arose between Paul and Barnabas. It served to advance the gospel, restore a brother, and support the ministry of both members of the missional dispute. The legacy of this sharp division is a series of positive statements about the life, ministry, and value of all the members involved. One searches in vain for bad-mouthing or criticisms. We would do well to learn from their lesson.

OUR CONVICTIONS SHOULD OPERATIONALIZE OUR BELIEFS, NOT WEAPONIZE THEM

This book argues for convictions because convictions move our beliefs into action. They unpack our beliefs and move them into our daily lives—one might say they operationalize our beliefs.

But one of the ways things go wrong is when our convictions weaponize our beliefs instead of operationalizing them. Weaponizing a conviction involves two things: making it powerful and applying it to others. We usually amp up the power by associating our conviction with a belief of transcendent importance—such as a doctrine that defines the faith, like the incarnation, the resurrection, the Trinity, or the authority of Scripture. If, for example, our conviction operationalizes our belief about the Trinity, we tend to think it *is* a belief about the Trinity. Once our thinking has taken this turn, we take the second step of weaponization and apply our amped-up conviction to others. We associate our conviction with the Trinity, and therefore, everyone else must associate it with the Trinity. Consequently, anyone who denies our conviction is also denying the Trinity—a classic and definitional mark of heresy.

To offer an illustration, let's consider the intriguing differences in the reasoning behind a single position that some evangelicals have taken on gender roles. Note that in this example, we are not considering people with conflicting convictions but rather people who share a conviction but arrived at it by different reasoning. Some complementarians see gender roles as a matter of church polity, grounded in biblical teachings about the leadership of local congregations. Others see gender roles as a matter related to biblical anthropology and appeal to biblical teaching about the nature of human beings as male and female. Still others see this as a matter related to trinitarian theology using analogies from biblical teaching about functional subordination in the Godhead. Though everyone in this example has the same convictions about gender roles, one person sees the issue as a debate about *ecclesiology*, while another person sees it as a debate about theological *anthropology*, and a third sees it is a debate about the *trinitarian theology*. All appeal to biblical teaching, but the one who regards it as a matter of church polity might readily agree that this is a "disputable issue" and happily give grace to those who see it another way. But for the one who sees this as a matter of trinitarian theology, it is a matter of heresy since it relates to one's doctrine of the Trinity.

Notice what has happened. Once one's beliefs about gender roles are associated with one's beliefs about the Trinity, it is easy for the gender roles issue to become "weaponized." There may be nothing wrong with anchoring one's beliefs about gender roles in one's understanding of the Trinity. However, it is important to make *explicit* the connection between these two different concepts. It is not a direct connection but rather one that is born of analogies. The relationship of the Father to the Son is used as an *analogy* to the relationship between a husband and a wife or a man and a woman. The analogy has scriptural support but is still an analogy, and an analogy is never an identity.

In fact, the trinitarian implication of this analogy stirred quite a controversy in 2016. Opponents of the trinitarian reasoning given above objected that it falsely appealed to the "eternal functional subordination" of the Son—in effect, the claim that the Son was functionally subordinate to the Father even before his incarnation. But subordination means subordination of the will. Therefore, it is argued, eternal functional subordination requires that the Father and the Son had two different wills *before* Christ became incarnate, an unusual position to take. Furthermore, this position assumes the relationship between those wills would best be described as the Son's will eternally submitting to the Father's will. This might be a way to describe the Son's *human* will in the incarnation, but this seems a strange way to describe the Son's divine will in relation to the Father's divine will throughout eternity. As theologian Fred Sanders states: "I would never say the eternal Son obeys the eternal Father, or that a structure of command and obedience characterizes the divine being."[3] So, in effect, overplaying the analogy between Trinity and gender roles may have had the side effect of denying an orthodox trinitarian Christology.

These arguments were rebutted by those on the other side. This book is not written to solve this particular controversy. The importance for our current discussion is simply the difficulty that comes from weaponizing a conviction—upgrading a conviction about gender roles into a conviction about the Trinity. There are simply too many elements in the chain of reasoning that moves from a confessional belief about the Godhead to a guideline of conduct regarding gender roles. The two items cannot be equated.

Weaponizing is particularly important to mention in a chapter about church divisions. Dividing the body of Christ should never be done lightly. However, one of the few times that we are quick to do it is when someone is denying a doctrine like the deity of Christ or the Trinity. These are so clearly defining confessional beliefs of the faith that we are pretty quick to justify a split. Unfortunately, when we weaponize our positions by not only *attaching* them to such high-level doctrinal beliefs but *equating* them with these beliefs, we are suddenly prone to divide the body when the issue at stake would ordinarily not lead us to do this.

5

CROSSCULTURAL INTERLUDE

OF TATTOOS AND ADULTERY

Conflicting convictions are a bad enough problem within a single local church that shares a common culture. When we start crossing cultural boundaries, the problems become even more radical. Consider this story from Amy Medina, an American missionary in Tanzania describing an experience her husband (Gil) had as a teacher in a Bible college there:

> Gil taught a class on developing a biblical worldview. . . .
> Something came up about tattoos, which was met by a
> strong negative response by the entire class. Gil was in-
> trigued by this, so he posed the question, "Which would
> bother you more: If your pastor got a tattoo, or if your pastor
> committed adultery?"
>
> Unanimously, the class agreed that a tattoo would be much
> more disturbing. Of course, this led to a lively conversation. . . .
> Another American missionary was visiting that day, and when
> he told the class that his two adult (Christian) children both

had tattoos, the students were dumbfounded. Gil and our visitor were dumbfounded that they were dumbfounded.[1]

For Christians in America, these beliefs seem strange to the point of being mistaken and highly problematic. Why are these students adamant and unanimous that tattoos are worse than adultery? It is easy to consider this just another instance of syncretism or the gospel failing to penetrate a culture fully, but let's avoid the quick dismissal. Let's trace these moral judgments across the spectrum of convictions described in the previous chapters. Imagine that you asked the Tanzanian students to explain the underlying roots of their convictions. Let's consider three different stories that you might hear in response to your inquiry.

The students explain that there is an explicit command of Scripture that forbids tattoos (Lev 19:28), just as there is an explicit command of Scripture that forbids adultery (Deut 5:18). The real issue, as they see it, is *not* how Tanzanians rank the importance of two different commands, both of which they believe to be binding, but rather why Americans think one command is binding and the other is *completely irrelevant!*

The students explain that tattoos are associated with witchcraft and evil spirits. A tattoo, regardless of personal intentions, is a mark of ownership placed on your body that either confirms the influence of a witch doctor or an evil spirit over your life, or at the very least implies or invites such influence. Adultery is wrong, but surely even Americans think it is worse for a pastor to publicly identify with an evil spirit.

The students explain that both are wrong, but adultery is usually handled outside of the public eye so that it does not bring shame to the wife or family or to the church as a whole. Tattoos, on the other hand, are visible signs of allegiance to evil spirits or tribal witch doctors. Culturally, the tattoo proclaims that Jesus is not really my Lord—some other person or spirit is. No Christian should be making such a statement, particularly not in such a publicly visible way.

These answers would likely give most Americans pause for thought. Clearly there is more going on in this discussion than we first imagined, and clearly the Tanzanian students are sensitive to some biblical issues like spiritual warfare to which Americans often pay comparatively little attention. Let's run these answers through the spectrum of conviction.

The first response anchors the students' convictions in their confessional belief of the authority of Scripture. In this case, Scripture offers a moral mandate in the form of two commands. To disobey either of these commands is to disobey Jesus—calling into question either the authority of Scripture or the lordship of Christ. The students are not superstitious or unlearned; rather, they are trying to be devout and faithful to Scripture. In fact, they wonder why Americans refuse to honor the biblical command. No doubt the Americans would affirm their commitment to Scripture but stress the importance of proper interpretation. Principles for applying biblical commands across historical and cultural contexts would have to be addressed. Also, distinguishing old and new covenants bears on this question. For example, some dietary regulations from Leviticus are explicitly *not* mandated under the new covenant. Indeed, it is striking how similar these issues are to the underlying issues of days and diets in Romans 14. Once everything is on the table, we discover that this is not a conflict about confessional beliefs or moral mandates but rather about principles related to details of biblical interpretation regarding Old Testament commands, not the authority of Scripture itself. Applying the conviction spectrum helps us to find common ground and also clarify what our differences really are.

In the second and third responses, the focus is on spiritual warfare rather than biblical interpretation. The Tanzanian students are not so much concerned with a biblical command against tattoos but rather are concerned about the influence of demons and supernatural evil. Surely the allegiance of one's heart to Jesus is the most important question every Christian must answer. Getting a tattoo is a public sign that marks one's allegiance as lying elsewhere than with Jesus—perhaps to a tribal witch doctor or to an evil spirit or some other supernatural evil. Adultery is a moral failure, but it is not in and of itself a transfer of allegiance from Christ to Satan. An American might protest that no such thing is intended by a tattoo and that the students are simply reading Tanzanian cultural concerns into an American tattoo. The Tanzanians may well feel that the Americans are simply unaware of the dynamics of spiritual warfare. They may also worry that the Americans are deluding themselves by thinking that their ignorance offers some sort of protection to the spiritual peril that they see so clearly. The Americans might very well say the same things about the peril of downplaying the spiritual significance of adultery. In this case, the controversy seems to be over core values: the importance of spiritual warfare as opposed to the importance of sexual fidelity.

Also looming in the second and especially the third approach to this controversy are differing values of honor and shame within the community. The public flaunting of a tattoo that questions one's allegiance to Christ seems to be highhanded and offensive to the community at large. The condition and effects of adultery—at least adultery that is kept private—can be repented of and hopefully rectified without bringing public shame to those involved. Americans may have a hard time seeing it this way, but this probably reflects a tendency to evaluate actions more on a guilt/innocence model, asking if an action is in accordance with a moral law. Tanzanians probably evaluate actions more on an honor/shame model, asking if an action brings shame or honor to oneself and one's community. It is important to note that these different models of evaluating an action are not completely separate from one another. Both cultures understand both models to an extent, but, in this case, guilt before the law as opposed to shame before the community is *valued* differently in the two cultures.

To conclude this discussion, let's identify some of the benefits that come from approaching a disagreement by thinking through the conviction spectrum:

1. The conviction spectrum helps identify where the conflict is actually located. It also helps us find common ground from which to work. In this case, despite doubts at the outset, the conviction spectrum revealed that both groups share a common commitment to the authority of Scripture and the obligation to honor its commands.

2. The conviction spectrum also helps us identify key points of difference, differences that vary for the multiple suggested responses from the Tanzanian students. In some cases, the key difference relates to interpreting and applying commands of the Old and New Testaments. In the other cases, the differences focused more on core values reflected in different importance placed on spiritual warfare and sexual fidelity and honor and shame within a community.

Finally, it should be stated that real differences remain. The conviction spectrum does not eliminate disagreements but rather locates and clarifies our disagreements. The goal is that appreciating the common ground lays a foundation for respecting differing convictions. This opens the door to further conversation and hopefully to respectful compromises along the lines which Paul suggests when he exhorts those who are stronger in faith not to flaunt their freedom and those who are weaker in faith not to judge their brothers.

6

HOW UNITY
IS THREATENED

You can buy one for $38.99 and have it the next day via Amazon Prime. The portable smoke machine comes with LED lights and a wireless remote control. In minutes a church auditorium is filled with a fine mist augmented by bright colors. An inexpensive way to liven up a room and create ambience. Sounds fairly harmless.

Yet, for one church it almost split them apart. The first Sunday someone turned on a smoke machine, heated conversations ensued.

One group argues that just as a microphone amplifies sound a smoke machine simply amplifies light during worship. An opposing group asserts that mist and colored lights turn worship into a concert. If our goal is to attract non-Christians, comes the retort, then what's wrong with putting on a concert? It might make visitors feel comfortable! Some are incredulous: So, worship has now been reduced to entertainment? Quickly, opinions harden. $38.99 is all it takes to create relational fissures.

We use the example of a smoke machine not only because it almost split this church but also for how quickly and passionately people judged its use. Some say it's *completely* inappropriate, while others claim it's an attempt at being current. In fact, a friend of ours said a smoke machine is a bad example because the answer to it is so obvious—perhaps it was obvious to him but not all the people on the other side? Sadly, divisions are not limited to smoke machines. While researching this book, we became aware of divisions in churches, Christian organizations, and Christian universities caused by differing answers to the following questions:

- Which version of the Bible should be quoted from the pulpit?
- Is reciting the Jesus Prayer ("Lord Jesus Christ, Son of God, have mercy on me, a sinner.") supporting Catholic doctrine?
- To be welcoming, should we have gender-neutral bathrooms in our church?
- How seriously should a church take issues of diversity?
- Is it appropriate for Christian leaders to drink alcohol?
- Should our worship service be multigenerational? How can a pastor address adult topics with a nine-year-old in the audience?
- When organizational leaders are required to travel cross-country, can they travel first or business class? Is that good stewardship of donors' money?
- Is starting a homeless ministry going to bring unstable and potentially dangerous people into our community?
- Should a Christian marriage conference use a movie clip powerfully depicting marital conflict where one character says, "Oh, my God!" Isn't that violating the Fourth Commandment to not use God's name in vain?

What was your response to these provocative questions? Did you find yourself at times muttering, "How in the world is that a big deal? Who cares!" Conversely, did it surprise you how passionate you were about what should be the answer to certain questions? Did any biblical passages come to mind to augment your opinion? What makes conflict among Christians so difficult is that individuals and groups don't merely disagree but feel that the Bible supports their position. Often in Christian conflict each side tries to play the ultimate trump card: "The Bible clearly says . . . !"

How should Christians respond when unity is unexpectedly threatened via a smoke machine or a particular translation of the Bible and each side claims biblical warrant? In the following pages we'll consider the importance of protecting unity and understand from a communication perspective how divisions take root and escalate.

PAUL'S CALL TO UNITY

In the summer of 2019 both of us walked through the ruins of the ancient city of Ephesus during a trip to Turkey. The experience made Paul's challenge of nurturing a young Christian community come alive. Though only a remnant of it still exists today, Ephesus was once one of the most influential cities in Asia. City life was full of politics and commerce, all of which was done under the looming presence of the goddess Artemis. She was the religious heart and soul of the city reflected by the temple dedicated to her. Her temple—with sixty-foot columns—was four times the size of the Parthenon in Athens. New Testament scholar Clint Arnold asserts that her influence cannot be overstated. "The temple was the major banking center for the city, her image adorned the coinage, a month of the year was named after her, Olympic-style games were held in her honor (called the Artemisia), and she was the trusted guardian and protector of the city."[1] Allegiance to Artemis, in short, was nonnegotiable.

Paul unequivocally instructs young believers in Ephesus to shun old allegiances. "So I tell you this, and insist on it in the Lord, that you must no longer live as the Gentiles do, in the futility of their thinking" (Eph 4:17). Paul understands that adherence to such a command will put his readers on a collision course with a city entrenched in the worship of Artemis. The key to survival will be their unity.

"Make every effort," states Paul, "to keep the unity of the Spirit through the bond of peace" (Eph 4:3). In the original Greek, Paul's word choice is even more dramatic. The word *effort* (*spoudazō*) carries the idea of determined exertion. Unity is hard work, and Paul is imploring his readers to marshal their full energy to staying unified. Similarly, the word *keep* (*tēreō*) suggests we exercise watchful care over unity as though it was a priceless possession.[2]

What's concerning is how quickly we ignore Paul's admonishment when conflict surfaces. Rather than putting in the time and effort to protect unity, our first inclination is to often leave or desubscribe when faced with conflict or differing opinions.

Each year my university invites faculty to participate in the Lent Project by submitting online devotionals centering on specific passages. I (Tim) selected a passage where Peter describes Jesus' reaction to being reviled (1 Pet 2:22-25). To illustrate what reviling must feel like for a person of great status, I referenced President Trump being publicly mocked on *Saturday Night Live* through Alec Baldwin's harsh impersonation of him in which he suggests the president is stupid.[3] I knew it was risky but thought the parallels between human and divine status could be helpful. Many not only found it unhelpful but offensive. "Why would you do that? I am aghast! I consider it unconscionable to create any kind of parallel between an unrepentant adulterer and the Lord of Life! I am unsubscribing!"

Reading their responses, two thoughts occurred to me. First, I chose to follow up individually with those who unsubscribed, but only one was willing to engage me. Second, the unity Paul describes will be weakened if our first response to controversy or conflict is to disengage rather than put in the work to guard it. In the end, unity may not be salvageable, yet it is only to be abandoned after our full effort is given. If you are going to voice a complaint, at least be willing to hear a response.

According to Paul, what are the ingredients that comprise giving it our full effort? Throughout his letter to the Ephesians Paul mentions key relational traits such as humility, gentleness, and patience (4:2), putting off falsehood (v. 25), anger management (v. 26), and edifying speech (v. 29). One trait has particular bearing on our discussion of easily disengaging when offended: long-suffering. When hurt by another, Paul admonishes us to exhibit patience by "bearing with one another in love" (v. 2). This phrase is alluding to the person who, having been injured by another, "does not suffer himself easily to be provoked by them, or to blaze up in anger."[4] It is particularly in those situations where we feel provoked or injured—either by a harsh comment or a seemingly insensitive Lent devotional—that we need to double our efforts to resist anger and pursue the offender. Paul understood that in a city dominated by pagan worship Christian unity would be essential and must be doggedly pursued.

A BREACH IN UNITY

All of us know what it feels like to experience conflict within an organization, university, or church. People we once felt close to now seem distant and even angry. Individuals we used to be excited to see are viewed with suspicion. What most of us many times don't understand is *how* the conflict started and gained such momentum. Renowned British anthropologist Victor Turner spent his lifetime studying how diverse communities build cohesiveness through the use of symbols, rituals, and shared expectations. Specifically, Turner was interested how communities handled potential rifts that might— if left unaddressed—threaten the entire community. Over time, he came to identify a clear progression of how conflict starts and gain momentum. The four distinguishable phases are: *breach, crisis, redress,* and either *reintegration* or *schism.*

Breach. A breach occurs when some established norm, rule, or expectation has been ignored or purposely violated. A breach can be overt or merely the deliberate nonfulfilling of a norm. Turner notes that a dramatic breach "may be made by an individual certainly, but he always acts, or believes he acts, on behalf of other parties, whether they are aware of it or not. He sees himself as a representative, not as a lone hand."[5] A breach can happen within a small group, between groups, or encompass an entire community. Regardless of the group's size, some basic principles can be gleaned from Turner.

First, a community, organization, or church must be aware of communal norms and expectations. When I attend this church or plan a campus event, what *spoken* expectations (as stated in a faculty handbook, student code of conduct, or church doctrinal statement) or *unspoken* expectations (appropriate style of dress, what speech is unacceptable, or how to voice disagreement during a sermon) are there?

Second, what happens when well-established norms are suddenly violated or changed? Who had the power to alter these norms, and what input did the overall community have in ratifying these changes? Are the steps to changing norms known by all? And, does everyone have equal access to evoke change?

Third, a breach is usually centered on what Turner calls a "symbolic trigger" that gives expression to the altering of communal norms. Symbolic triggers are anything that signals to one group the changing of a norm, rule, or expectation. Consider these possible triggers:

- To cut cost, faculty parking spots are eliminated on campus.
- To make an auditorium more contemporary, a large pipe organ is covered with a silk screen.
- Annual raises are suspended during dark economic times.
- Administration will no longer reimburse meals at academic conferences.
- Due to its neo-Marxist roots, the term *social justice* will no longer be used.
- The Enneagram is banned due to dubious origins.
- The pastoral teaching team announces they now affirm same-sex marriages.

How did each one of these statements strike you? How do you think your friends would respond? If enough of your friends are upset, is it worth doing something about it? Before planning a response, it's crucial to determine what the severity of the breach is. Is banning the Enneagram the same as church leadership affirming same-sex marriage? While that question may seem silly, it's important to go back to the discussion we had in chapter 2 on Paul's discussion on days, diets, and convictions. To summarize, Paul identifies *confessional beliefs* (deity of Christ; salvation in Christ alone; abstaining from orgies, drunkenness, and sexual immorality); *matters of taste* (listening to secular music, choosing to homeschool, responsibly drinking alcohol); and *disputable matters* (which biblical translation is most accurate, how to define divine sovereignty, what role should social justice play in evangelism) where Christians can legitimately disagree over important issues. Is a smoke machine a matter of taste while supporting a pro-life candidate is a *confessional belief?* The answer is not simple and will be determined by the group to which you belong. In turn, your group's perspective will equally determine if a breach or crisis has formed?

For example, if a smoke machine is viewed as merely a *matter of taste*, then many options are open to a community, such as creating multiple services and giving people a choice. If people are opposed to mist and colored lights, then pick a service that doesn't utilize them. If a church only has one worship service, then is it possible to alternate its use with more traditional services? However, what if a seemingly innocent smoke machine is interpreted as something that conflicts with a *confessional belief?* What if this machine is seen by some as a symbol of worldliness? After all, doesn't Paul command us to "not conform to the pattern of this world" (Rom 12:2) because, in part, "this world in its present form is passing away" (1 Cor 7:31). Surely, worldliness is not merely a matter of taste but a moral mandate of Scripture. How a group rhetorically frames an issue will determine their willingness to embrace compromises or middle ground.

Crisis. Once a breach has been interpreted by one group as a crisis, what's to be done? Before acting, it would be wise for any group to consider the following: Are we correct in our interpretation of the breach? Has it reached crisis proportions? Are we open to the fact we could be wrong? Is the concern of our group strong enough for us to alert other groups? How will coalition building be seen by leadership? If an opposing group is to be engaged, what is the best way to communicate our concerns? Last, what if no one will take our concerns seriously?

Turner asserts that if a crisis continues to escalate, it can have two powerful effects on a community. First, crisis becomes a turning point where a "true state of affairs is revealed, when it is least easy to don masks or pretend that there is nothing rotten in the village."[6] Forcing a community to deal with a breach may serve as a diagnostic to assess overall relational or organizational health. Communication consultant Patrick Lencioni suggests that many organizations exhibit "artificial harmony," which he describes as "a system in which different perspectives are either suppressed by team leaders or glossed over, and yes-men go back to their own divisions to deride executive team decisions, fueling silos, inward thinking and infighting."[7]

Second, once a breach has been labeled as a crisis, there is no turning back. The crisis "takes up its menacing stance in the forum itself and, as it were, dares the representatives of order to grapple with it. It cannot be ignored or wished away."[8] Inherently, crisis carries with it a sense of risk since feelings or opinions once shared cannot easily be taken back.

Last, if addressed properly, conflict can strengthen a community or organization by surfacing latent conflict, revisiting relational norms, rebuilding trust, creating ways to resolve or manage disagreements, and promoting perspective-taking.

Redress. Once a crisis has been acknowledged it can be dealt with in a number of different ways. Turner notes these means may "range from personal advice and informal mediation or arbitration to formal juridical and legal machinery."[9] Redressing a crisis can be done either informally or through more official means.

Informal. Occasionally a crisis can be addressed by a simple conversation between individuals who represent opposing groups. Rather than presenting the grievance to a superior, or the elder board, a causal conversation may be effective. We remember a colleague telling us of a special meeting convened at his university to address a thorny disagreement between two noted theologians. A dinner was organized where the two were to have a moderated discussion to air their differences. When the day arrived, the conference room was packed with faculty being turned away for fear of violating the fire code. Through an odd stroke of luck (or providence) the two scholars found themselves sitting next to each other. Our friend sat at the table next to them, his back almost touching the chair of one of the scholars. Everyone—our friend included—fully expected to witness pre-discussion fireworks.

Unexpectedly, the room was filled with their boisterous discussion and, surprisingly, laughter. The two found out they shared the same sporting interests, favorite movies, and sense of humor. And, over dinner they unearthed some unexpected areas of agreement. "Long before this debate," stated one of the scholars when he got up to speak, "we should have grabbed a meal. I don't think we are all that far apart!" *Really?* One meal, and a theological crisis is averted!

For five years, I (Tim) served as the chair of Biola's Media Board. In part, the board served as a mediator when issues arose concerning our campus newspaper, magazine, television station, and radio. If a person or group felt slighted or misrepresented through a media outlet, the board could be called. I can't tell you how many times I received an angry email requesting—even demanding—the board convene to hear a grievance. My standard response was to first set up a coffee between an editor or producer and a person representing a group who felt slighted. Only one instance in five years failed to produce a resolution. Jesus is wise to suggest that if you find yourself at odds with another person go to him or her "just between the two of you" (Mt 18:15).

In each instance where resolution was achieved, compromise of some kind was required; but for compromise to occur, both sides need to acknowledge the concern of others. Nicole Roccas wisely notes that, "all of human development can be summed up as the process of learning we are not the sole protagonist in the story—other people exist."[10] Unfortunately, informal channels do not always work. Jesus also recognizes that there will be times when a one-on-one conversation will fail and others will need to be brought in (Mt 18:16).

Formal. Anyone who has ever worked for an organization, church, or university understands that conflict is inevitable. In fact, organizational communication scholars Papa, Daniels, and Spiker state "conflict between members is an expected reality."[11] Subsequently, every organization must have mechanisms in place where grievances can be aired, such as a human resources department or an elder board. Turner wisely notes that not all communities are adequately prepared to handle a crisis. Thus, members must ask "Whether the redressive machinery is capable of handling crises" and is equipped "to restore peace among contending groups. And if not, why not?"[12]

It would be naive to think all redressive mechanisms are equally effective in impartially investigating complaints. Though a CEO, J. T. O'Donnell surprisingly writes in her blog that "HR is not your friend." She continues: "Therefore, when an employee comes to HR with a negative claim or issue, HR's first thought is, 'How do I minimize the impact of this on the entire organization?'"[13] Surprisingly, one of the benefits of a crisis is that it surfaces the level of confidence a community or organization has in its redressive mechanisms.

Ideally, Christian redressive mechanisms ought to especially garner trust. To do so, Paul informs Titus that anyone who aspires to be an overseer must, in part, be "hospitable, loving what is good, sensible, just, devout, self-controlled, holding fast the faithful word which is in accordance with the teaching, so that he will be able both to exhort in sound doctrine and to refute those who contradict" (Titus 1:8-9 NASB).[14] Leaders who exhibit such qualities would in turn promote trust among those they lead.

While we fully support anyone who feels the need to seek formal means to address conflict, our present focus is to equip opposing groups to have productive conversations before including leadership.

Reintegration or schism. This last phase acknowledges two possible outcomes to a crisis. Either the "disturbed social group" will be re-integrated back into the community, or there will be a recognition of an "irreparable schism between contesting parties."[15] We understand that in matters of conviction (core doctrinal beliefs), dis-agreement will most likely entail the removal of one party. All our university faculty are given academic freedom to pursue personal convictions concerning theology or political issues. However, we also are required to sign a doctrinal statement each year. If personal theological beliefs clash with our doctrinal statement, then a schism has surfaced and it's time for a faculty member to move on.

It is also possible that separation may also be required in matters of taste or dispute. Over time it may become apparent that a par-ticular church or organization has moved in a different direction that no longer aligns with your convictions or priorities. Rather than spending time and energy trying to change the priorities of the majority, it may be time to find a community or organization that is a better fit.

Is reintegration possible if two groups cannot see eye to eye on disputable matters? The answer depends on what redressive mecha-nisms a church or Christian university has in place and if both parties will choose to submit.

Imagine an adult fellowship in your church concludes that a second dwelling of the Spirit—as evidenced by speaking in tongues—is necessary for a believer to fully mature in his or her faith. They believe that this conviction should be adopted by church leadership and affirmed from the pulpit. The church elders have written a position paper on this issue stating that none of the supernatural gifts or signs of the Spirit are endorsed nor prohibited. The leaders of the adult fellowship ask to meet with church leaders and elders to ask the position paper be rewritten to reflect their views. The elders state they are happy to hear from the group and a meeting is set up.

After the meeting the elders thank the group for a thoughtful and biblical presentation. A week later church leadership announces that they will not alter their position. "Can we still teach in our adult fellowship our view of the necessity of supernatural gifts of the Spirit?" ask the leaders. No. If the group is sponsored by the church or meets on church grounds, leadership requests that this conviction not be shared or endorsed by the group's leaders. The elders explain that this doesn't mean that individuals from the group cannot have conversations with other parishioners outside the group concerning this disputable issue. In fact, the church encourages all members to have healthy disagreements with each other. Yet, what if the decision does not sit well with leaders of the adult fellowship? What are they to do? At this point it would be wise for members of the group to seek the Spirit and ask if they can—in good conscience—abide by the decision of the elders. Do the benefits of this church body outweigh the disappointing decision rendered by leadership?

While in college I (Tim) attended a dynamic church led by a gifted senior pastor. During one sermon he posited the idea that while it was impossible for a true believer of Jesus to lose his or her faith, the writer of Hebrews seems to suggest that one could consciously give up one's faith and become apostate. This renouncing of faith is irredeemable since God knows the person will never return. I was surprised and disappointed to hear his provocative view. A week later we met for coffee where I fully intended to announce I was leaving the church. I could see the disappointment on his face when I told him I felt compelled to leave.

His response surprised me. After assuring me that this was not an official doctrine of the church, he asked: "Can't we merely disagree? Don't all the good things the church is doing give you reason to stay?" He was right. I was deeply involved in our church's homeless mission and evangelism training program. Thus, we agreed to disagree. I stayed at the church, and we often had spirited conversations about this disputable matter. Though neither of us have changed our stance, we have maintained a healthy admiration for each other through the years.

Let's complicate matters more by returning to our scenario of an adult fellowship group wanting to affirm the necessity of supernatural signs and gifts. Imagine another group wants church leadership to affirm from the pulpit the exact opposite—that speaking in tongues is not only unnecessary for sanctification but is mostly demonic in origin. They too ask to meet with church leadership. The meeting is granted, resulting in a decision that in the opinion of the elders speaking in tongues is not demonic. In fact, the elders believe the exact opposite—speaking in tongues, while not necessary for mature faith, can be experienced by a believer. This opinion does not sit well with members of this group. They too are asked to seek the Spirit as to whether they can abide by this decision.

The key for both groups is determining if this issue is an absolute or a disputable matter where good people can disagree. If it is a matter of confessional beliefs or an absolute moral mandate, then perhaps it may be time to find another church or body of believers that share a similar view. However, if both groups see it as a disputable matter and decide to stay, they must adhere to Paul's admonition to "get rid of all bitterness, rage and anger, brawling and slander, along with every form of malice" (Eph 4:31). This does not mean that groups cannot disagree with each other, but their communication must exhibit kindness and compassion as modeled by Christ (v. 32). Equally, each group must not only abide by the elders' decision but refrain from seeking to undermine that leadership overtly or covertly. If these qualifications are met, then groups—even though disappointed with a particular decision—can be reintegrated back into the church body.[16]

CONCLUSION

In the blockbuster horror movie *Us*, Jordan Peele creates a world where humanity is broken up into two groups: individuals who live aboveground in affluence and individuals called the Tethered who live below in impoverished tunnels. This frightening world is predicated on one simple rule: whatever decisions are made by those aboveground are forced upon those living underground. When families aboveground enjoy a feast during Thanksgiving, those underground are forced to eat a poor version called "raw rabbit." Peele's point is that we—regardless of race, gender, or politics—are all tethered to each other.

Paul makes a similar point to his readers in Ephesus. He reminds them that they have been called into "one body" of believers (Eph 4:4). In a city flooded with pagan temples, there was only *one* church. Like it or not, they are all tethered together. How one group (Jews) acts will undoubtedly impact the other (Gentiles). Unlike Peele's terrifying vision of social classes, Christians living with status or resources are compelled to consider how those God-given resources must be used for the benefit of all Jesus followers. When crisis comes, this tethered group must overcome racial, ethnic, gender, and social differences for the good of all. In the following chapters, we share strategies rooted in communication theory and the Scriptures that will help us resolve our differences and protect our most sacred possession—unity.

7

PERCEPTION IS REALITY

"Be glad your mother didn't murder you!"

The person yelling made direct eye contact with me (Tim). I've never been the target of such raw emotion. I looked down the long ramp leading out of the auditorium, and it was filled with protesters holding signs.

Some context may be helpful.

While on staff with Cru (formerly Campus Crusade for Christ), I was part of a Christian think tank called the Communication Center. In part, we trained Cru staff on how to effectively communicate the Christian worldview to an increasingly diverse culture. At the same time, I was just beginning my graduate education in communication theory and learning about key concepts such as perspective-taking—purposefully seeing the world through the eyes of another. Skimming through the local newspaper during lunch, a coworker informed me that a pro-choice conference was being held the next day in our city.

"I would love to be a fly on the wall and hear how they frame the issue and talk about us pro-lifers," my friend said casually.

"Let's go," I replied. "Instead of imagining what others think, let's hear it firsthand. Maybe we'll be surprised."

The next day we were unexpectedly sitting in the opening session. What shocked me was how similar it was to many Christian conferences I attended—songs, impassioned speakers, and a lot of interesting people. I was pleasantly surprised how the vitriol was kept to a minimum when talking about the religious pro-life camp into which my friend and I were firmly entrenched.

As late registrations, we were sitting in the back of the auditorium and were the first to leave the building at the end of the day.

"If you don't want your baby, we'll take her!"

"Don't stop a beating heart!"

"God loves your baby!"

"Any way you cut it, it's still *murder*!!!"

The sidewalk leading out of the auditorium was transformed into a gauntlet of mostly antagonistic voices. We tried to engage a couple of people but were met with anger bordering on rage. In no way are we suggesting that this group represents all pro-life advocates, nor are we even suggesting that the entire group that day was full of anger. However, the section of protesters we encountered were aggressive, not interested in listening, and looking for a fight.

"How can you support women who choose to kill the innocent? Shame on you!"

"How do you know what I believe?" I tried to interject. "Maybe I'm just gathering information."

"What information do you need? Abortion is murder. Period!"

"What if we told you we are actually Christians," my friend said. "We're just trying to understand their point of view."

"Being at that meeting condones murder!" a woman interrupted.

"No Christian should set foot at a pro-choice rally," chimed in another person.

I began to respond, "But shouldn't we try to understand and listen to their—"

"*No Christian* should set foot at a pro-choice rally!" reiterated the man.

The more we attempted to explain our goal of perspective-taking, the more it seemed to anger them. Walking away I have never felt so utterly misunderstood. I naively thought that once they learned we were fellow Christ followers equally committed to the sanctity of life, the tone of the conversation would change and their perspective would be altered. Nothing could have been further from the truth. One of the most complex truths of communication is our perception of people and events *determines our reality*. Once created, our perception is extremely difficult to change. Learning we were on staff with Cru and actually helped train people how to present a pro-life position did nothing to change these protesters' negative perspective of us.

Can you imagine the tension if these people and I attended the same church? In the above situation, when the conversation died down we simply went our separate ways. Yet, what if Sunday came and we found ourselves sitting in the same sanctuary, separated by a few rows of pews? While committed to a pro-life stance, we no doubt disagree *how* we should best advocate our position—organize protests at pro-choice rallies or engage in perspective-taking by seeking out those with whom we disagree? How easily our perceptions of each other could further sour fueling a potential breach. Add to this tension the reality that many Christians in our pews maintain a pro-life conviction and also identify as Democrat—some of the most pro-life advocates we know have been lifelong Democrats. The goal of *Winsome Conviction* is to somehow find a way to balance differing expressions of a conviction—protest or perspective-taking, Democrat or Republican—in a way that doesn't splinter the church.

If we are to effectively help navigate breaches that challenge unity, then we'll need to know how perspectives are formed, fortified, and most importantly, altered when necessary.

HOW PERCEPTIONS ARE FORMED

Communication scholar G. A. Quattrone notes that perception of those with whom we disagree consists of *categorization, characterization,* and *correction*.[1] When we first meet a person from a different group we immediately place him or her into broad categories such as liberal or conservative, loyal or disloyal, faithful or heretic, and so on. Once placed into a category, we assign specific characteristics to that person. The oft-neglected correction stage occurs only if we get to know those individuals and address inaccurate judgments. Quattrone urges group members to ask crucial questions: Is our characterization of other groups accurate? How much has our perception been influenced by bias, misinformation, or hurt feelings? How can we check the perception we have of others? Is our description of others completely negative? If so, how can we correct our views to make them more nuanced or balanced? Each of Quattrone's categories deserves our attention.

Categorization. Through the growth of the internet, laptop computers, sophisticated mobile phones, and ubiquitous news programs, we receive five times more information in one day than people did in 1986![2] How can we possibly think deeply about all the people or situations we encounter in a daily avalanche of information? We create elaborate ways to conserve energy by becoming *cognitive misers.* Just as a miser spends as little money as possible, cognitive misers spend as little mental capital as possible when judging people. The more time it takes to elaborately interpret people and place them in nuanced mental categories, the more exhausted we become. So, we use mental tools to cut corners.

Prototypes. A prototype is the clearest expression of a category. Think of the worst teacher you've ever had at any grade level. Does one come readily to mind? Mine (Tim) was an earth science professor who wore pullover golf shirts that didn't fully cover everything. As he talked about layers of sediment (dirt), he would rock back and forth—his shirt moving increasingly upward, exposing more skin. As a theater major uninterested in science, it was torture. As I progressed through years of graduate school, this professor became the prototype of a boring professor by which all others are judged. Even today, when I listen to a person give a TED talk or watch a lecture online and start to think a person is boring, I compare them to this particular professor. Suddenly, some speakers seem not as boring as I first thought. In order to quickly judge people or situations, we create prototypes for the worst or best family vacation, the worst or best date, the worst or best roommate, movie, boss, pastor, parent, presidential candidate, church, and so forth. As soon as we meet a person, we judge them according to a corresponding prototype.

Stereotypes. Stereotypes are predictive judgments we make based on an entire group. In our second year of marriage, my wife and I lived overseas for a year in the former Soviet Union. Before our trip I had never met nor had a conversation with a Russian. Yet I still had impressions of Russians based on how they were described in news programs, history books, novels, or even popular movies like *Rocky IV*, where Rocky Balboa fights a Russian boxer, Ivan Drago, who is scientifically engineered to be a killer. All of these portrayals— good and bad—created a crude expectation for me of how a Russian *should* act. And while stereotypes are not inherently wrong or even negative, in today's caustic communication climate, we are flooded with the negative general impressions of others.

Snap judgments. While we are often taught not to judge a book by its cover, we quickly size up people—consciously and unconsciously— and assign them personality traits. The key is that these judgments happen instantaneously and are binary. You meet someone and immediately assess: attractive/unattractive, funny/lacks humor, leader/ follower, artistic/uncreative, boisterous/reserved, romantic potential/ merely friend, committed/uncommitted, godly/lukewarm, and so forth.

The danger with snap judgments is how much our current context—mood, physical condition, or frame of reference—can bias our judgments. Researchers at the University of Waterloo in Canada concluded that "in a happy atmosphere, we tend to judge a face with a negative expression positively; conversely, when we are immersed in a dismal atmosphere, a happy, lively face can provoke a negative reaction."[3] The subjectivity of our snap judgments or first impressions necessitates verifying the accuracy of the categories we place people in.

In today's complex and diverse world, we need to hold our categories loosely, knowing that people don't always neatly fit into categories—there are such people as conservative Southern Baptist feminists, celibate gay Republicans, and Democrats for Life.[4] Interestingly, how would Jesus fit our modern categories? Alexandria Ocasio-Cortez—affectionally known as AOC to her supporters—argues that Jesus today would be negatively categorized as an unseemly radical. "If Christ himself walked through these doors and said what he said thousands of years ago—that we should love our neighbor and our enemy, that we should welcome the stranger, fight for the least of us, that it is easier for a camel to go through the eye of a needle than for a rich man to get into a kingdom of heaven—he would be maligned as a radical and rejected from these doors."[5] Her implied question is a thoughtful one: Are the religious categories we've constructed ones that Jesus himself could adhere to? It is easy for our categories to convey false characteristics.

Characterization. On a PowerPoint slide I (Tim) put the following categories: professor, feminist, student athlete, postmodern, Trump supporter, transgendered, pro-choice advocate, older sibling, Trump detractor, sophomores, adjunct faculty, vegans, White supremacist, Gen Z.

"Write down three characteristics of each group," I instructed my students.

They quickly write down their impressions. What's interesting is that while many have never met a self-professing White supremacist or self-described feminist, they have impressions of each category. The feminist prompt often garners from my conservative students responses such as angry, anti-man, bra-burner, committed, lesbian, passionate, Lady Gaga, #MeToo, activists, and scary. While their responses include some positive qualities—committed, passionate, activists—it is still generally negative. The point is that our categories are not value free, but rather each category is colored with implicit bias and discrimination.

Our bias toward certain groups or categories was on full display when pop sensation Taylor Swift released her single, "You Need to Calm Down." While Swift received kudos for advocating a toning down of the harsh rhetoric that often surrounds social issues like LGBTQ rights, she made it clear what she thought of one particular category—anti-gay protesters. In her award-winning music video, LGBTQ celebrities joyfully dance as angry protesters—dressed in flannel, wearing trucker hats, and sporting bad teeth—hold crude signs: Adam & Eve, not Steve! Get a brain morons. Homosexuality is a SIN! Apparently for Swift, the category of LGBTQ supporters is rich and full of nuance, while anti–gay rights people are characteristically angry, ugly, and uneducated. The irony of admirably addressing the negative stereotypes of one group while vilifying another was not lost on Dave Holmes, who sarcastically wrote for *Esquire*: "If there's one thing that has been shown to get through to homophobes, it is casting them as ugly and poorly-educated. They take it to heart and it works every single time and it is a shame more people don't do this."[6]

While most of us suspect we are continually being categorized and characterized by others, there are times when it is blatantly obvious. A few years ago, I (Tim) took part in a one-day event designed to improve today's political discourse. When you registered, you had to state your political affiliation, to which I put independent. Everyone attending was assigned a colored name placard—red for Republican or blue for Democrat. I later learned that there was no provision for independents, and a color was randomly assigned.

I put on my blue lanyard and walked into the main session. It was the oddest feeling to have a person walk up to me and immediately glance at my color. If it was a fellow blue, I was welcomed and the conversation quickly shifted to an assessment of the event. In one glance, it was assumed how I felt about major political issues. When a red walked up to me and saw my color, there was often an overt attempt to be pleasant. After the perfunctory greetings, however, the conversation would quickly turn to his probing of stances assumed to be mine.

Throughout the day I found myself wondering: How often are the categories I quickly place people into—based on politics, gender, race, religion—in need of correction? While correction is the hardest stage, Quattrone asserts it is essential.

Correction. This oft-neglected stage happens when we engage in *perception checking*—asking a person to confirm or disconfirm our views of them. I previously mentioned a controversial Lent devotional asking people to imagine what it must be like for President Trump to face public ridicule at the hands of the cast of *Saturday Night Live*. For readers who objected, I was quickly placed into several categories—either a Trump supporter/sympathizer or a quasi-blasphemer comparing a crass womanizer to our Savior. During an in-depth email correspondence with a disgruntled reader, I was able to correct perceptions and offer my rationale for using one public figure to understand another. Some of my corrections were embraced and others were debated. However, I was allowed to directly address concerns another had of me.

How often do we intentionally allow people a chance to directly address our characterizations of them? The ancient writers who comprise the book of Proverbs remind us that in a dispute we are often swayed by a particular opinion until "someone comes forward and cross-examines" (18:17). The correction stage is a crucial opportunity to allow our perceptions of others to be cross-examined or challenged. How many misunderstandings could be avoided by informing others of our perception of them and inviting a response or clarification? However, please remember that a clarification is not a cross-examination and a spouse or friend is not a witness. A trial lawyer often uses questions to strategically lead a witness in a particular direction, while in a conversation we lower our defenses and invite the introspection of others.

Quattrone's three-stage process is helpful in understanding in broad strokes how we form impressions of others. How are those impressions—snap judgments—played out in real time?

THE DEFINITION OF THE SITUATION

Communication scholars utilize a helpful process called the definition of the situation, which is comprised of three questions we ask ourselves during an encounter: What beliefs do I have about myself? What do I believe about the other person? What are we trying to do together? The following scenario may be instructive.

After giving an exam, I go over answers with my students. When we come to one difficult section a student raises her hand: "Dr. Muehlhoff, I found question number ten overly specific and even unfair! You were trying to trick us!" Before her objection is even finished I begin to ask myself questions.

What do I believe about myself? I've been creating tests for more than twenty years and think my exams, while difficult, are fair. I would never purposefully write an unfair question designed to mislead students.

What do I believe about the other person? While trying to remain objective, her insinuation that one of my questions was *un*fair bothers me. My immediate thought is that at *best* she's challenging my test-writing ability; at *worst* she's questioning my integrity. In front of the entire class, she's calling me out.

What are we trying to do together? Since I've adopted a negative interpretation of her, I now view her question as a challenge to my character.

While the above scenario is negative, we could easily imagine a different set of interpretations on my part. A student frames her question identical to the first scenario casting my question as suspect. Except this time I know the person raising the objection. I've had her in a several classes and know her to be a good student who cares about her grades.

What do I believe about myself? I still believe I am a competent professor who writes fair tests.

What do I believe about the other person? Based on previous interactions with her—and the quality work she's done—I believe she respects me and enjoys my classes. Thus, I interpret her question as a sign she is perhaps stressed about her grade. She doesn't mean to be disrespectful; she's frustrated.

What are we trying to do together? A good student cares about her grade and is wanting clarification from her professor on a particularly difficult question. She may not have (according to me) asked the question in the best way, but she has every right to ask for clarification. Often students questioning my exams have perceptively surfaced deficiencies in my tests. It's amazing how many times I can look at a question and think it's legitimate, only to find later through the probing of my students that it didn't make sense or was flat-out wrong!

Notice that in this second scenario nothing changed except *my* interpretation of her—and, that my answering of these questions shapes the *entire* tone of the conversation. Communication scholars assert that the definition of the situation is the backdrop of all of our interactions with a spouse, child, family member, coworker, neighbor, and most importantly for our consideration, a fellow Christian. As we are conversing with a person we are asking and answering these three crucial questions in real time, and *how* we answer colors the entire exchange. The definition of the situation also serves as a diagnostic we can use to learn about ourselves.

Beliefs I have about myself. Before a conversation even begins, what's your assessment of yourself? Are you ultra-confident in your knowledge of issues, people, or the Scriptures? Or, do you often second-guess yourself when embroiled in a disagreement with others? As the conversation intensifies, do you back away, deferring to the other person? The following questions may help uncover general beliefs you carry into conversations:

- Am I secure with my level of education?
- Am I up-to-date on current issues or what's happening around me?

- In what areas am I most confident to discuss with others?
- In what areas am I least confident?
- If a conversation turns to spiritual matters, how well do I know the Scriptures?
- How often during a discussion am I convinced that my view is correct?
- After a conversation, how much do I second-guess myself?
- Do I view myself as a kind person?
- How proficient am I at speaking the truth in love?

The answers to these questions—and many more—determine your general mindset about yourself as you head into a conversation. For example, one of the hazards of having a PhD is that I'm usually convinced that I'm right when disagreeing with others. Therefore, when defining the situation, the beliefs about myself— especially if the topic turns to politics, theology, or sports (college football in particular)—is that in the end my view will prevail. I'm not saying that it always does, but my assuredness seldom wavers.

Beliefs I have about other people. Equally important are the beliefs I have about other people. Consider these diagnostic questions:

- Am I a good judge of other people?
- How quick am I to judge the intentions of others?
- What general biases do I have that might throw off my assessment of others?
- How complex is my view of other people?
- Do most people exhibit goodwill in disagreements?
- Are there general stereotypes that I tend to buy into?
- Do people generally twist facts to make a point?
- How quick am I to judge a person's educational level?
- Are there certain topics that make objectivity difficult?

What we are trying to do together. An awareness of the personal beliefs we harbor and how we tend to approach others powerfully shapes how we view our interactions. When it comes to theological disputes, the definition of the situation becomes particularly relevant.

The importance of taking steps to understand how others perceive us is creatively called *world-traveling* by cultural critic Maria Lugones. She states that a world "need not be a construction of a whole society. It may be a construction of a tiny portion of a particular society. It may be inhabited by just a few people."[7] To travel to another world is to understand how you have been constructed in the eyes of others. To travel to another person's world does not mean that you condone the view you may encounter. "There may be worlds that construct me in ways that I do not even understand or I may not accept the construction as an account of myself."[8] World-traveling is an exercise that can surface powerful stereotypes. For herself, Lugones notes that she often enters a world that constructs her as "stereotypical Latin."[9] To enter another person's world—even if it's filled with hurtful stereotypes—is both risky and, according to Lugones, an act of love. For Christians, world-traveling can not only be a powerful form of perspective-taking but a crucial first step in cultivating unity.

TEST CASE: DISAGREEING OVER GENESIS

Since long before the infamous Scopes Monkey Trial of 1925, Christians have clashed over evolution. Integrating evolutional theory with Genesis has been seen by religious conservatives as a fool's endeavor. However, Christian scientists, philosophers, and theologians continue to interpret Genesis in a way that—according to them—squares with seemingly indisputable evidence supporting evolution.[10] Battle lines have been drawn within the Christian community, and discussions quickly turn ugly. Is it possible for Christians on opposite sides of this issue to change negative perceptions of each other?

Todd Wood and Darrel Falk are committed Christian scientists who have radically divergent views when it comes to evolution and faith. Darrel is the senior adviser for BioLogos and a self-described Christian evolutionist, while Todd is the founder and president of

Core Academy of Science, which promotes a young-earth creationist perspective. While both had known of each other for years, they had never met. Their opportunity came when leaders from the Colossian Forum—a group dedicated to tearing downs walls between Christians—set up a weekend meeting. Their encounter is the subject matter of the book *The Fool and the Heretic*, which surfaces the principles of perception we've been considering.

Categories and characteristics. As Todd and Darrel prepare to meet, they've already put each other in specific categories. While Darrel acknowledges his opponent loves Jesus, he puts him into the category of *pseudoscientist*. Even before the conversation starts, Darrel confidently states that his side will prevail "because the evidence for evolution is vastly overwhelming" and any serious scientist would acknowledge it.[11] Todd equally acknowledges Darrel's faith commitment but puts him in the category of *pseudoheretic*. He explains why young-earth creationists are so passionate about opposing people like Darrel is that he is "challenging the foundation of the Christian faith."[12]

As if these categories weren't inflammatory enough, they are filled with derisive characteristics. Pseudoscientists are people of faith who deeply weaken the ethos of the church by placing a literal interpretation of Genesis above and against a clear expression of God's general revelation—indisputable scientific evidence for evolution. Darrel forcefully states that "Christians who embrace and promote young-earth creationism are contributing to the dismissal of Christianity within the scientific and academic communities, and because those institutions wield so much influence over all of culture, it is not an overstatement to say that young-earth creationist movement presents a barrier to the gospel to many."[13] For many young-earth creationists, pseudoheretics like Darrel casually—and even at times gleefully—dismantle the traditional interpretation of Genesis that provides confidence to Christians worldwide. At the heart of the Genesis account is a probing question: Can we trust the clarity of the creation account? If evolution is true, asserts Todd, then trust in the Scriptures has been compromised.

You can imagine how placing each other in such caustic categories would make dialogue between Darrel and Todd difficult bordering on impossible. Todd recognizes this reality and candidly admits that "Darrel is basically the archenemy of young-age creationists!"[14] He continues, "This is not a minor spat where we can agree to disagree, hug each other, and move on. On this important topic of origins, we are mortal enemies."[15]

During their pivotal first meeting we see how the categories they've created for each other shape how they define what the other is trying to do. Darrel suggests that young-earth creationists only give lip service to science but aren't serious scientists. Todd vividly recalls Darrel's condescending claim: "It wasn't long into our discussion that he suggested that I don't really know science. I won't go into the details, but I remember thinking, 'Here we go again.'"[16] For young-earth creationists, this is an all too familiar response: "This is what so many Christian evolutionists do. Instead of taking me seriously as a scientist and listening to what I have to say, they fall back on the idea that I must be a fool for questioning evolution."[17]

At this point, Todd sternly informs Darrel that not only did his doctoral and postdoctoral work—at distinguished universities—focus on evolutionary biology, but that he's been a member of the Society for Molecular Biology and Evolution as long as he's been a member of the Creation Research Society. Looking right at Darrel, he concludes, "How much more study of evolution do I have to do?"[18] With tension rising, they agree to call it a day.

Correction. Back in his room, Darrel has a decision to make. Does he allow this new information—Todd's intentional study of evolution—to alter his impression, or does he set it aside and hold onto his negative categories of pseudoscientists? Upon reflection, Darrel comes to two conclusions. First, he had been too aggressive in tone with Todd at the start. What was fueling his angry posture toward Todd? Second, and most importantly, he had grossly underestimated Todd's level of education and knowledge of evolution. "I was just plain wrong," he flatly states. "Todd regularly attended the

annual meeting of the Society of Evolutionary Biologists. Not only
did he understand evolutionary theory quite well, he likely knew it
better than me."[19] Not only does Darrel make corrections in his
perception of Todd, but he shocks everyone by what he does the
next morning—issuing a public apology to Todd.

Todd recalls this surprising development. "Humbly and with
emotion in front of the same group that had heard him be so
casually dismissive, he admitted that he was wrong and that I really
did know a lot about evolution. He even admitted that what he said
about my science was dumb." Darrel's humility made a lasting
impression. "I've gotten used to being unfairly criticized, even ridi-
culed. What I'm not accustomed to is having an evolutionist apol-
ogize to me."[20] One of the key results of the correction stage was a
decision on Todd's part to continue the conversation. "I agreed to
a second meeting with Darrel."[21]

A few observations about this interaction are worth noting. First,
though not having ever met each other, Todd and Darrel had already placed each other in negative categories that primed each
other for disagreement. Second, based on these negative impressions, they confidently knew what the other person was doing
during their first exchange (definition of the situation). Darrel was
arrogantly adhering to evolutionary theory as he dismantled traditional views of Genesis, while Todd was destroying the ethos of the
church by ignoring the indisputable evidence of evolution. Third,
despite such negative views of each other, the oft-neglected correction stage surprisingly occurred. But why? What moved Darrel
to alter his opinion? Learning that Todd belonged to an organization he greatly respected—the Society for Molecular Biology and
Evolution—increased Todd's credibility. Don't miss this key point—
garnering respect from a person is hard work, takes time, and entails personal sacrifice. Can you imagine all the presentations Todd
listened to at these proevolution conferences that made his skin
crawl? I'm sure he wanted, on many occasions, to leave and never
come back. Yet his membership and participation changed the

impression of his "arch enemy" toward him. Are we equally willing to put in the hard work of changing people's impressions of us?

CONCLUSION

Reading the exchange between these two Christian scientists fortified our conviction of the central role perceptions play in the communication process. Humans are prone to categorize one another, but these categories often include negative characteristics. As Christians, we ought to be careful how quickly we stereotype each other. Christian author Eugene Peterson reminds us that each person is uniquely made in God's image and often full of surprises. Thus, stereotypes or broad labels are only a starting point. He writes, "Labels are marginally useful for understanding some aspect of human condition, but the moment they are used to identify a person, they obscure the very thing that we as pastors are most interested in, the unprecedented, unrepeatable soul addressed by God." Moving from categorization to correction allows a person to self-identify and show his or her uniqueness. Peterson continues: "I am always a little impatient and try to fit them into categories that I am familiar with, so I won't have to take the extra time to get to know them. I have, after all, a lot to do."[22]

To be honest, the correction stage is often messy and takes a lot of work. We like having our world figured out via carefully orchestrated categories. To allow a person the opportunity to correct our assumptions is often scary and could have lasting consequences. Who knows how the debate over evolution has been altered by Darrel and Todd's willingness to push into the correction stage?

One comment by Todd has made a lasting impression on us. Reflecting on his time with Darrell he concludes: "Christians rarely disagree together, and that's hurting the church just as much as the disagreement itself."[23] Why do we become entrenched in our perceptions and categories, rendering dialogue undesirable? In the next chapter we discuss how the groups we belong to can— unwittingly—become isolation chambers.

8

FELLOWSHIP GROUPS OR ECHO CHAMBERS?

I stop in my tracks.

It's as if I have walked into an invisible force field—I can't move.

While in college, some of my (Tim's) friends saw a killer sale was happening at a local sports store. We all needed new basketball shoes, and after class we set out. Outside the store were signs "Half-off shoes" and "Buy one, get one free!" My friends walked right in; I stood outside unable to move. Off to the side, one man stood with a sign: "Unfair wages! Workers on strike!" The store was packed with people coming and going, and this sole figure barely made eye contact with anyone.

But I saw his sign. I couldn't go in.

Growing up in East Detroit, my dad worked in the auto industry. Every morning at 4:30 a.m., my dad carpooled with other men to a factory to put in twelve-hour shifts. In addition to hard work and mouths to feed, what all these men had in common was that they were proud union members. When strikes against management happened, I remember waking up to milk, food, and money left on our doorstep from union organizers. It was all we had to get through the week.

"Son, you never cross a man's picket line unless you have to!" my dad said, maintaining firm eye contact.

Shoes didn't seem like a good enough reason, so I stood outside as my friends scored on deals. They felt no guilt because they grew up in different cities immersed in different communities—different groups yielded disparate convictions. Groups play a vital role in how we relate to ourselves and others. "Every segment of our society— from the largest multinational organization to the political workings of federal, state, city, and local governments to the smallest community action group to friendship groups to the nuclear and extended family—relies on groups to make important decisions, socialize members, satisfy needs, and the like."[1]

Take a minute and think of all the diverse groups you belong to and interact with during the week? Don't limit interactions to people you physically meet with, but rather, think of all the groups you electronically belong to or check in with. Does the number surprise you?

THE CENTRALITY OF GROUPS

Researchers have long noted that we have—since the first humans— sought out tribes or groups to belong to. Oxford anthropologist Robin Dunbar noted that individuals in diverse societies all seem to gravitate toward groups of thirty-five to fifty people, which he labeled as "bands" or "overnight groups." These groups hunted to-gether, ate together, and slept in the same proximity. Dunbar also noted that these bands developed ties to other nearby groups forming a "village" of roughly one to two hundred people. It wasn't that these villages regularly hunted or ate together but rather joined each other for certain rituals or special occasions. While each village didn't know everyone, they did interact enough on a regular basis to cultivate strong bonds via rituals, or festivals. In ad-dition, villages regularly grouped with other villages to form "tribes" ranging from five hundred to two thousand people. While these tribes provided a sense of unity and strength, people had an interesting reaction—they tended to cling to their own bands. Why? Dunbar concluded that the human brain has a cognitive limit of how many acquaintances we can cultivate at one time: 150. This number—regardless of the size of a community, university, corporation, or church—seems to hold firm. So much so, Dunbar's findings are now simply known as *Dunbar's number*.[2] In short, this number represents a cognitive limit to the number of people you can maintain a relationship with where you are familiar with each person and understand how that person relates to you and the entire group.

The implication of Dunbar's findings is significant for leaders who seek to cultivate unity within a church or a Christian organization such as a university or corporation. The very people we try to lead on a macro level will naturally seek out small bands or groups that will greatly shape how they perceive the church or university as a whole. If Dunbar's number holds, then we'll place a cognitive limit of roughly 150 people on the groups to which we belong. Keep in mind that Dunbar's number represents the limit and does not mean that we'll all belong to groups of that size. In fact, some of us may have a much lower capacity—thus, smaller bands. Yet each group, regardless of size, will form its own communication climate, rules, norms, and culture. Knowing the powerful pull of creating groups within larger communities, it's crucial we understand what these groups do and the impact they have on each of us.

WHAT GROUPS DO FOR US

What does our participation in groups provide? The groups we adhere to offer us several key benefits.

Groups help us flourish. Research is overwhelming that social isolation is devastating to us mentally, emotionally, physically, and spiritually. A 2015 study from Brigham Young University found that being disconnected from groups or communities was *as* detrimental to our overall health as obesity (the top precursor to heart disease) or smoking (the number one contributor to lung cancer).[3] It seems that God has hardwired the human soul to be part of a group or community. After all, Adam was told by God himself that being alone was not good, and one key aspect of the creation mandate was to be fruitful and multiply (Gen 1:28). In John's euphoric vision, heaven is presented as a city full of human activity and diverse groups of all kinds (Rev 21). In contrast, C. S. Lewis in his classic *The Great Divorce* presents hell as a place where people are constantly—and eternally—moving *away* from each other.

Groups provide interpretive communities. In the previous chapter we introduced readers to a communication tool called the definition of the situation, which helps us interpret the actions of others. However, how we apply this tool is greatly shaped by biases, perspectives, and values of the groups we immerse ourselves in. The power of groups to sway our perspective was dramatically on display during the trial of Trayvon Martin.

On the night of February 26, 2016, in Sanford, Florida, George Zimmerman, a volunteer neighborhood watch captain, fatally shot seventeen-year-old high school student Trayvon Martin. Zimmerman, sporting a bloody nose and head wounds, claimed he was attacked and defensively shot his unarmed assailant. Zimmerman was charged with second-degree murder but was later acquitted. After the verdict, CNN correspondent Tom Foreman identified the role groups played in interpreting this racially charged incident:

> To one side, Zimmerman was at worst an overzealous citizen just trying to make sure his neighborhood was safe. To the other, he was a gun-toting predator, hunting, harassing and provoking a fatal fight with an innocent teen. To one side, Martin was little more than a child returning home after getting a snack. To the other, he was a hulking young man who could have gone inside, talked with Zimmerman or called the police, but instead decided to attack with his fists and paid with his life.[4]

Notice Foreman's use of the plural when he observes that "one side" viewed it a particular way. He notes that the interpretation offered by elements of the African American community clashed with those offered by elements of the White community.

And since people on both sides seemed to have decided the case before the testimony was heard, the verdict was bound to be disturbing no matter how it tilted. Simply put, preconceived notions effectively had people watching two different trials, with every bit of testimony and evidence producing different, and often opposing, reactions in those dueling audiences.[5]

What's interesting about the above example is the reaction it received from readers of an early draft of this book. Two separate readers argued that in the tragic killing of Trayvon Martin there was only *one* side. Ironically, each picked a different side and excluded the other. They both stated in their own ways, "This is a bad example because clearly one person was completely justified in his actions." Yet they both seemingly missed Foreman's point as he described the trial: dueling audiences were watching two different trials. Foreman was not arguing that the two perspectives were equally moral or equally valid but simply that both views were embedded in and sustained by preexisting groups, not just isolated individuals.

Differing interpretive communities play a significant role in how disagreements between Christians get played out. With all of our claims of individualism, our interpretations of controversies will be greatly swayed by the group we have invested in— their collective opinion will deeply impact our own. In healthy groups, the interpretive lens we receive will be robust and full of diverse perspectives.

Alarmingly, some join groups precisely not to be exposed to differing viewpoints. MIT scholar Sherry Turkle coined the term "communal narcissism" to describe how we are often compelled to join groups that allow us to avoid people we disagree with or find annoying.[6] Rather than being challenged or having mental horizons expanded, cognitive misers conserve mental and emotional energy by surrounding themselves with people who think like they do!

Groups help us effectively solve problems. Group decision making—when done in a healthy manner—can help provide a structure where individuals collectively help break down complex issues.

In a West Coast community, residents and law enforcement agencies are increasingly concerned with homeless camps of two hundred or more individuals being set up along beach areas. Their concern is fueled by seemingly daily accounts of violence between homeless individuals, rampant drug use, unsanitary conditions, and vandalism within surrounding neighborhoods. The decision is made to disperse the camps, creating a crisis for homeless residents. Where will they go? As the day draws near, local churches have a decision to make: Do we temporarily house the homeless or not?

At one church, leadership decides to respond by opening its doors to homeless individuals until a permanent solution can be found. Unfortunately, one morning a homeless man wanders off campus and walks into a house and looks in on a woman taking a shower. The violation felt by this woman, surrounding community, and church members was palpable. At a town hall meeting church leadership is asked to defend its decision. Before the meeting, groups within the church find themselves at odds with each other. One group argues that the chief responsibility of church leadership is to protect the flock from both spiritual and physical danger (1 Pet 5:2). Another group asserts that neighbor love as prescribed by Jesus (Mt 22:37-40) compels us to reach out to those in need even if it involves risk. Which group is right? The benefits of group decision making is that it provides guidelines for moving forward in addressing conflict.

Step 1: Description of problem. As clearly as possible, what is the nature of the problem? Is the problem one of fact (How much money will it take to minister to the homeless? Do we have adequate systems in place to do so?), value (What is the worth of something?

Does the value of safety trump the value of helping others?), or policy (What criteria are we using to decide if we should help? Are the criteria clear enough to make future situations about other social issues?). Using members within your group to describe the problem helps create a layered approach difficult for one person to replicate.

Step 2: Brainstorm potential solutions. What are the many ways our church could respond to this crisis? Possible solutions could include: (1) remaining uninvolved and allowing local government to act; (2) opening our doors to as many as possible as we increase church security; (3) while not directly housing the homeless, raising funds that allow community groups or governmental agencies to act; and (4) not responding to this particular crisis but making sure to develop criteria that balance safety needs with being good neighbors and lay the groundwork to respond to future needs. The key to this step is not to prematurely judge any one idea. Stage two simply entails listing all possible suggestions—even ones that may rankle you or your group. In this crucial stage, all options should be considered. A key mistake we'll consider later in the chapter is how groups often ignore legitimate options held by outside groups.

Step 3: Expound and evaluate each possible solution. Communication theorists understand that *acknowledgment* is a key element in a healthy communication climate. Acknowledging the strengths of a position before judging it will help affirm those in your group who support a particular option. What makes this step potentially volatile is if individuals within a group feel their option was not given full consideration or presented as passionately as other options. This stage could possibly entail inviting members of other groups who hold different opinions to come and explain their ideas and solutions.

Step 4: Coming to a final decision. Of all the possible options, which most represents the values and convictions of our particular group? As much as possible, a final decision needs to balance the convictions of all groups that comprise the church or university. How do we protect our own yet still adhere to Jesus' command to love our neighbor? If we open our doors, how can we assure all groups that their safety needs will be respected? What does implementing our plan look like in practical terms? Where will funds come from, or who will carry out our decision (e.g., church staff, volunteers, church community groups)?

Step 5: How do we present our ideas to leadership? What avenues of communication with leadership are available to our group? Once a meeting with leadership is arranged, what is the best way to communicate our group's convictions and plan of action? If we think this particular issue has reached crisis levels, how do we convey this concern? How will our group respond if leadership rejects our plan? While group decision making offers many benefits, it does come with risk.

WHEN GROUPS GO BAD

How is it possible that brilliant individuals often collectively make bad and even disastrous decisions? How can obvious counter-evidence or differing perspectives be ignored? These questions haunted Yale psychologist Irving Janis as he studied the political process that led to a failure to protect Pearl Harbor during World War II, the poorly organized Bay of Pigs invasion in 1961, and the unwavering belief by political and military leaders that the war in Vietnam was winnable. The result is a concept that changed how we view the ability of a group to make well-informed decisions. The term *groupthink* is so prevalent today that Yale political scientist Donald Green argues that it comes up at least once a day in conversations between colleagues and students.

Janis defined groupthink as a situation where participants "adhered to group norms and pressures toward uniformity, even when their policy was working badly and had unintended consequences that disturbed the conscience of the members." In short, "members consider loyalty to the group the highest form of morality."[7] While volumes have been written about groupthink, it would be wise to consider key signs that it may be occurring in your church or Christian organization and how to prevent it.

SYMPTOMS OF GROUPTHINK

Overestimate the ability of the group. When your church or organization faces key struggles or differences of opinion, groups quickly form to address the issue at hand. As mentioned in the previous chapter, groups powerfully shape how an issue or the definition of the situation is interpreted. It's good that groups within the church care about the issue and want to address it. However, groupthink starts to take root when individuals think the opinions of the group are *all* that is needed. Why do we need to consult others? We have gifted people in our group that can more than adequately address this issue in a fair and balanced manner.

In part, this overconfidence is spurred on by an unwavering confidence that all relevant information can be gleaned from internet searches. No doubt the internet has helped much in making information accessible to any searcher. However, it has also had some unexpected results. First, why talk to an expert when we can google hundreds of experts? However, sloppy internet searches place informed and uninformed sources side by side, where each seems to have an equal ethos. Does a person really need to have a PhD to know about an issue? In his provocative book, *The Death of Expertise*, Tom Nichols argues that the quality of an opinion ought to matter. "I fear we are witnessing the *death of the ideal of expertise itself*, a Google-fueled, Wikipedia-based, blog-sodden collapse of any division between professionals and laypeople, students and teachers, knowers and wonderers—in other words, between those of any achievement in an area and those with none at all."[8]

Second, over time our internet searches—through complex search filters and algorithms—start to shape our searches with similar results and sources, limiting our scope of knowledge rather than enhancing it. Researchers at the University of Michigan School of Information note, "collectively, these filters will isolate people in information bubbles only partly of their own choosing, and the inaccurate beliefs they form as a result may be difficult to correct."[9]

To be clear, using the internet to do research does not necessarily promote groupthink. It's when consulting only fellow group members or seeking out online sources rather than engaging educated views of people within your church or community can fuel a false sense of confidence. Overestimating the resources of your group paves the way to the most dangerous aspect of groupthink—closedmindedness.

Isolated groups. Due to an overestimation of the group's ability to address a crisis, groups become increasingly isolated from other groups. All conversations become in-house discussions. While deliberation is key to group decision making, groupthink emerges when differing perspectives are not only avoided but unwelcome. Such isolation often breeds harsh stereotypes of other groups. When outside perspectives are ignored it greatly skews Quattrone's three-step process—stereotypes and negative categories are free to grow without opposition, and the correction stage never materializes.

Since the people being talked about are not present, harsh rhetoric is often used to describe them without objection. Before I (Tim) pursued graduate education in communication theory, I worked on an MA in biblical studies from a Reformed seminary. Though not Reformed, I found the classes stimulating but also fertile ground for groupthink. During one class, a student asked the professor, "What should be done about the sin of Arminianism?" As the professor began his answer I raised my hand. "The sin of Arminianism?" I asked. "Isn't that unfair?" Realizing that not every student held his theological beliefs, he backtracked and agreed it was wrong to refer to a different theological system held by many quality biblical scholars as sin. However, if I had not been present, the claim would have stood. Groupthink occurs when dissenting positions are no longer presented because everyone assumes they are in lockstep with each other.[10]

Why are groups often so opposed to seeking out other perspectives? When groups slowly become entrenched in the belief they are right on a particular issue, opening yourself to alternative perspectives is risky. If we open ourselves to opposing views, what if some of our group are persuaded? Groups are right to acknowledge that opening ourselves to opposing views can bring about change in attitudes or convictions.

At age five, Megan would stand holding a sign that read in crude spray-painted words, "Gays are worthy of death!" She was too young to read the sign but knew it would garner approval from her parents and ten siblings. As a member of the radical Westboro Baptist Church, she was immersed in groupthink where a few faithful were right and everyone else was damned. In 2009, Westboro expanded its tactics and utilized Twitter to get the message out. Megan, now a young woman, found the tactic had unexpected results. As she engaged in "digital brawls," she found not all she communicated with wanted to fight. Some chose civility and a willingness to hear her life's story. One person, David, even came to visit her on the picket line to put a face on a Twitter handle. The result: for the first time she started to question her indoctrination. How is it possible our small family is right and *everyone* else is wrong? Are there no good counter arguments? Over time, these questions wore on her, resulting in her not only leaving the church but marrying David.[11] While this story is a salient example of the power of civility and compassion, it strikes terror into groups immersed in groupthink. *See, she exposed herself to outside voices and was converted,* the thinking goes. *And, it didn't take much—simply engaging in Twitter conversations.* Subsequently, people immersed in groupthink oppose even conversing with those on the other side. It should be noted that this type of intellectual isolation is not merely relegated to your group or church. It's indeed possible that entire denominations or political parties could adhere to an isolationist stance and view engaging the other side as weakness or even betrayal.

Loyalty is the highest value. Many argue that the central tenet of groupthink is its valuing loyalty above all else. When a group adopts a life-or-death approach to an issue within your church, the litmus test for the group is unwavering commitment. To waver or offer objections is seen as promoting disloyalty bordering on betrayal. Former President Barack Obama describes the dangers of what he calls a circular firing squad.

> One of the things I do worry about sometimes among progressives in the United States, maybe it's true here as well, is a certain kind of rigidity where we say, "Ah, I'm sorry, this is how it's gonna be." And then we start sometimes creating what's called a circular firing squad where you start shooting at your allies because one of them is straying from purity on the issues. And when that happens, typically the overall effort and movement weakens.[12]

When a crisis is facing your church or organization and your group alone has the answer, then any opposition or hesitancy to get on board is seen as straying from the purity of the cause and a firing squad is quickly formed. When rigid categories of us versus them are created, any offering of goodwill is viewed with contempt.

PREVENTING GROUPTHINK

If your group exhibits signs of groupthink, how can they be counteracted? The following suggestions may help.

Select a leader who solicits differing opinions. Does the leader of your group not only welcome differing viewpoints but seek them out? How does she react to those who object to the direction your group is heading? One summer I worked for a supervisor who, when faced with a differing opinion, would quietly let out a sigh. While barely audible, it communicated volumes. *I'm listening, but I disapprove.* Over time, objections became fewer and fewer.

How does a leader solicit contrary views? First, create a means by which group members can offer opinions anonymously. As a professor, when I want to really ascertain how my course is going, I'll ask students to submit their feedback through evaluations submitted with no names attached. These comments—both good and bad—offer honest insight into the wide range of student opinions. Select a leader who wants to hear all opinions of the group while protecting identities. Second, a leader can also ask certain members to specifically push back on the opinions of the group. I once worked on a complex project for an entire year. Just as the group was about to make our final recommendations to the administration, our group leader asked three of us to talk him out of the decision we were about to make. "Take the weekend and come up with your best counter arguments," he said. "You'll present them to the group on Monday." A leader who isn't afraid to receive pushback will in turn create a communication climate where others can voice concerns or objections.

Adopt rules in how you talk about other groups. "I thought my *rightness* condoned my *rudeness*," concluded Megan once she'd left the Westboro church. Megan's observation particularly seems to apply to Christians who feel they have theological rightness. Christian author John Stott notes that when some think they "smell heresy, their nose begins to twitch, their muscles ripple, and the light of battle enters their eye. They seem to enjoy nothing more than a fight."[13] Behind closed doors, how does your group talk about others when your nose starts to twitch? One of the key mistakes we make about communication is thinking it only exists on one level—our content (e.g., our arguments, words we use to convince others, the rhetoric we use to explain our view). However, communication theorists understand that the relational level—amount of respect, compassion, and acknowledgment—determines if the content can be received. Paul acknowledges both levels when he exhorts us to "speaking the truth [content] in love [relational]" (Eph 4:15). Peter echoes the same sentiment when he not only instructs us to be ready to offer a reason for the hope within us but also includes the relational—with gentleness and respect (1 Pet 3:15).

Sadly, Christians often focus merely on content and ignore the relational implications of what they say. At a pastor's conference hosted by his home church, popular Bible teacher John MacArthur participated in a panel where he was asked to give his first impression of a word offered by the moderator. Upon hearing "Beth Moore" (an equally popular Bible teacher), he immediately quipped, "Go home!" His answer garnered loud laughter and clapping from the audience. While MacArthur is certainly within his rights to argue that the Bible offers no justification for women preaching on Sunday mornings (content), he failed to take a respectful stance toward another public figure (relational).[14]

How does your group do in balancing both levels when talking about those with whom you disagree? In defining the situation, how charitable are you in interpreting what the other group is trying to accomplish? Do you exhibit compassion toward the emotions driving their actions? Do you acknowledge their concerns? Even as you disagree, is your language respectful? Having taught communication theory for over twenty-five years, I've become convinced of one simple truth: how you talk about people privately is how you'll treat them publicly. This is why Paul unequivocally commands us to replace bitterness, rage, anger, brawling, and slander (Eph 4:31) with tenderness and kindheartedness (Eph 4:32).

Invite feedback from outsiders. Is how you are interpreting the actions of others correct? Is your group creating one-dimensional stereotypes or nuanced views of others? How is your group coming across when presenting your ideas to others? One way to find answers is to invite outsiders to address your group. Once given access, these guests can offer invaluable perspective to the accuracy of your perspective. Rather than imagining what others think, allow people to speak for themselves.

The feedback and insights you garner from perspective-taking doesn't mean that you'll have to act on it. "Receiving it [feedback] well means engaging in the conversation skillfully and making thoughtful choices about whether and how to use the information and what you're learning."[15] Yet, what if the feedback offered contains valid arguments that challenge the core beliefs of the group? "It is true," asserts the founders of the Harvard Negotiation Project, "that a better understanding of their thinking may lead you to revise your own views about the merits of a situation. But that is not a cost of understanding their point of view, it is a benefit."[16] As followers of Jesus, our goal isn't to ensure our particular group holds on to power or wins at all costs. Rather, it's that we address a potentially divisive issue in a fair manner that ultimately brings honor to Christ. If your group is wrong on the particulars of an issue, better to receive it and make necessary corrections.

One last word on feedback—be wary of what you "hear" the other side is saying about you. Having been asked to mediate many disagreements at both the church and university level, it's shocking how many times a group will form negative impressions of other groups by things reported back to them second-hand. *I heard so-and-so said about your group. . . .* The ancient writers of the book of Proverbs are wise to warn that "the words of a gossip are like choice morsels; they go down to the inmost parts" (Prov 18:8). When hearing that another group is disparaging you, make sure to go directly to the source to gain better understanding. Rick and I once facilitated a conversation between faculty members where the central issue that was fueling conflict *never* happened! The anger one group had toward the other was over a gross mischaracterization of an event that happened on campus. However, to this day this event is still described by others containing this significant factual error. Verify comments before you allow them to shape the views your group has of others.

Keep the big picture in mind. For a group to exist it will necessarily create fences that distinguishes it from other groups. However, at all costs we are to try to avoid producing divisions that threaten unity. Those immersed in groupthink slowly adopt an attitude that better the church or university closes its doors than we lose this fight. The apostle Paul implores us to avoid such self-centered

thinking. Not only should we honor others, but we should steadfastly be devoted to each other spurred on by love (Rom 12:10).
What equitable situation can be achieved that honors—as much as
possible—the needs of the entire organization? Is it possible that
we can live and let live when it comes to differing positions?

If a group becomes toxic—leave. We are not suggesting that leaving
a group or community of believers is never warranted, nor easy.
Sometimes, the most Christ-honoring decision is to leave. There are
cases where individuals or groups have been so marginalized and
without access to power, that leaving is prudent.

What does your group do if you feel regularly ignored or even
abused by those in power? Your concerns are not only unwelcome
but are met with hostility. There is a significant difference between
hashing out disagreements within a healthy communication climate
and trying to shield yourself or loved ones from a toxic environment.
When things get toxic, leaving can be the most healthy option. We
want to be clear that a church making a decision that goes against
your desires does not in and of itself make the environment toxic.
However, refusing to acknowledge the concerns of a particular
group, or responding in hostility, can foster an unhealthy or toxic
communication environment. We've listened to many people describe the heart-breaking decision to leave a community they've
deeply invested in and loved but ultimately felt had become toxic.
Two friends recently described their ten-year experience at a church
as the nine *best* years of their life with the last being the *worst* due to
a change in leadership which they deemed unhealthy and antagonistic. In protest and with heavy hearts they decided to leave.

CONCLUSION

New Testament writers clearly understood the power of groups in
the furthering of the gospel. The majority of the letters are written
to churches in Corinth, Rome, Galatia, Ephesus, Philippi, Colossae,
and Thessalonica. Other letters, such as penned by Peter, are addressed to groups of Christians caught in the exile of "the Dispersion"

(1 Pet 1:1 ESV). Even the so-called "pastoral letters" addressed to Timothy and Titus are meant to be shared with groups of Christians. Yet, as mentioned earlier in the book, these groups of Christians started to form separate groups or cliques. Thus, Paul writes to the church at Corinth that he hears there are "divisions among you" (1 Cor 11:18). These groups were predicated on doctrinal differences or even on status, as to who baptized whom. Paul knew this was a serious threat and countered that while differences are real, we are still one body (1 Cor 12:12). His reminder equally applies to the tensions we feel today. The reality of groups *within* groups will be a challenge that will either strengthen the modern church or fracture us.

PUTTING IT ALL TOGETHER

9

POWER AND CIVILITY
IN A BROKEN SOCIETY

I do not distrust their motives; I distrust their power.
They have a lot of it.

PHILIP K. DICK

Philip K. Dick, a famous science fiction author, wrote these words as part of a critique of the dangers of living in a world where media, governments, large corporations, religious groups, and political groups can create what he called "pseudo-realities" and convey them right into our minds by electronic media. He points out that we often worry first about the motives of others, but sometimes the raw power, the hidden power, and the hidden exercise of the power are the real dangers.

Up to this point, our thoughts have centered more on people's motives—helping one another understand the reasons why we do what we do and believe what we believe. We think that promoting mutual understanding will go a long way to decreasing the vitriol that seems to be endemic in the public square and all too common even within the church. However, the issue of power cannot be disregarded. Our particular concern is not so much dictatorial leaders or coercive violence. These are certainly problematic, but they are also pretty obvious. Of concern to us is the more subtle way in which power in general and unequal power hierarchies in particular can damage the communication climate, corrode trust, hamper attempts at reconciliation, distort the truth, and ultimately lead to division and schisms which divide the body of Christ and destroy our public witness.

In this chapter we will discuss two different aspects of power. First we will consider what might be called "ordinary power." These issues arise around the identified authorities within a society as whole, as well as established authorities in a church or Christian organization. These authorities exercise power over the members of the group that is expressed in setting agendas, hiring and firing, making financial and missional decisions, and a host of other activities that they are appointed to do. Of course, there are times when this power is abused, but even when it is properly used, it can make for very challenging group dynamics when people are at odds with one another.

The other form of power, hidden power, is different. This form of power has become a major focus of academic and political reflection in the past few decades. It is the sort of power that is often at stake in discussions about social justice and is reflected in the ways in which the disenfranchised are treated by the elites and powerholders. In these cases there is a power imbalance, but the concern is not so much with the stated intentions of those in power as it is with the hidden agendas and unintended consequences of the decisions they make and the structures that uphold them. A similar conception of power is found in the New Testament passages referring to "the powers." Marva Dawn has offered an excellent discussion of these powers in which she emphasizes the pervasive and insidious nature of them exactly because they are diffused throughout the culture.[1] Their evil influence is exhibited in their capacity to control the imaginations and behavior of human beings individually and communally. Hidden power is often more influential in shaping our society than the tangible and visible expressions of ordinary power. It is also more problematic in disagreements between groups exactly because the hiddenness of hidden power means that one group or other may not actually see the power imbalance at all.

DYNAMICS OF ORDINARY POWER

If you wanted something to be done at your church or Christian organization, can you just do it, or do you need permission? If permission is needed, who are the power brokers that can grant or deny your request? Do you have access to these people? Will they listen to you? Do they listen to the concerns of the congregation equally? Or does it seem your leaders are biased toward a particular group or perspective? What should you do if your group is shut out, ignored, or even abused?

The leaders of your church or organization are largely responsible for creating *ideology*. Simply put, ideology is made up of the *ideas, values, beliefs*, and *convictions* that govern the behavior of your church. What is the ideology of your church or community? To surface it, do this thought experiment. Name three beliefs that are central to your church (e.g., We worship Jesus as God, we read and preach the Bible as God's Word, we feel there is salvation in no one other than Jesus"). Can you add three more? If so, what? What are the messages regularly sent by the church from up front or via announcements? What projects get funding? Right now, what ideas or convictions are there that you can't imagine being adopted? How do people in authority wield their power? Three common ways are through direct power, agenda setting, and voice.

Direct power. Direct power is simply the "ability to make others do what they would not do on their own."[2] Making others conform can be accomplished through establishing policies, rules, or criteria by which ideas can be considered or enacted. For example, a

Christian university may establish a code of conduct that prohibits drinking on campus or premarital sex. Students may or may not personally agree with the code of conduct, but the power to change it does not reside with them but rather with the board of trustees of the university.

One key result of direct power is the ability to shape how disagreeing with leaders is viewed by others. Geert Hofstede coined the phrase "power distance" to describe how people within a particular society acknowledge and accept an unequal distribution of power.[3] High power distance communities separate the powerful from those who lack power and even in some cases punish those who seek or challenge power. In contrast, low power distance cultures support the notion that challenging authority is not only acceptable but a sign of communal health. Community members are encouraged to challenge the status quo. How does the leadership in your church or organization view pushing back on their decisions?

Agenda setting. Leaders in your church or community have limited time and resources. While they may be aware of divergent views or needs in the body, they have to decide what is pressing enough to address. Do you and your group have the ability to get something placed on the official agenda? What methods are seen as legitimate ways to pressure leaders into putting your concerns on their radar? In one situation, a group whose views had seemingly been ignored by leadership decided to utilize Facebook to garner support. They created a Facebook page and explained their views and asked congregants to reach out to individual leaders to place them on the agenda. While the group felt empowered, leadership saw it as an inappropriate tactic to apply pressure.

Voice. Communication scholars note that *acknowledgment* is key to creating a positive communication climate. Do you feel leadership gives weight to the merits of your view? While acknowledgment is not synonymous with agreeing, it is a way to show that a perspective carries merit. A key part of voice is the ability to exercise it. While you may know the people who hold power (senior pastor, university board of directors, elders, advisory committee), will they recognize your voice? If leadership does recognize your voice, what constraints do they have the ability to place on you, such as time limits to present your view or in what form the communication must be delivered?

IS ANGER AN APPROPRIATE RESPONSE TO POWER?

Establishing rules and policies, setting agendas, hearing grievances, and settling disputes are all proper roles of those in leadership. However, the choices of those in power and their reaction to your concerns may have both disappointed you and made you angry. As a Christian, is anger ever an appropriate response? Perhaps. The Scriptures seem to suggest that anger can be appropriate, but it comes with risk. "In your anger," states the apostle Paul, "do not sin" (Eph 4:26). It seems that Paul is not condemning anger but rather laying out safeguards.

Christian thinkers such as Thomas Aquinas have long felt that anger is not inherently bad. In some situations, anger is an entirely appropriate and human response. Rebecca Konyndyk DeYoung, an Aquinas scholar, suggests that we must be "careful to distinguish anger, the *passion*, a part of normal human emotional makeup, from wrath, the *vice*, which is anger in its sinful, excessive, misdirected form."[4] Appropriate anger has as its goal the pursuit of justice, while wrath seeks to hurt others in an attempt to achieve a goal. Anger becomes warped when it "fights for its own selfish cause, not for justice, and when it fights dirty."[5] How can we advocate for justice while avoiding wrath and fighting dirty?

To the church at Ephesus, Paul gives a checklist of items that for him constitute dirty or destructive fighting and are to be abandoned at *all* costs. "Get rid of all bitterness, rage and anger, brawling and slander, along with every form of malice" (Eph 4:31). New Testament scholar Clint Arnold notes that in ancient literature bitterness, rage, and anger often appear together. The thought being that bitterness was an inward feeling of hardheartedness that a person feels toward another, fueling a response filled with anger and rage.[6] Paul adds malicious talk, which is denigrating or abusive speech meant to hurt another. Arnold concludes that believers "need to give focused attention to eliminating these ugly attitudes and behaviors from their lives. They are exceedingly destructive to community life."[7]

Is anger ever an appropriate response to those in power? Yes, if your anger is rooted in seeking justice and void of the negative characteristics listed by Paul. However, if your opposition to power consistently fuels rage resulting in your attempt to hurt those who have hurt you (malicious talk), then in pursuing your cause—however just—you have crossed a line. If malicious talk becomes the norm, then perhaps it's time to refrain from activism or leave. Conversely, you might be in a situation where leadership's response to your concerns or objections could be characterized by re-sentment, rage, and malicious talk. In that case, church leadership may need to be confronted—a possibility Paul himself acknowl-edges (1 Tim 5:19-20). In all cases, destructive anger must be care-fully managed. DeYoung offers a nice summary of the role anger plays in addressing unjust power: "Motivated by good anger, we hunger and thirst for righteousness, an appetite that depends on justice for its object, but on love for its right expression. Anger in these cases adds energy and passion to the execution of justice. The love that underlies it, however, keeps it in check, for love does not seek to destroy the other, but to set things right."[8]

It may seem that those resisting power are hopelessly hand-cuffed by Paul's scriptural prohibitions. The reality is that God cares about both the content level of our communication (our arguments and grievances) and the relational level, a concern consistently found in the admonitions of biblical writers. Paul commands us to speak the truth in love, while Peter instructs a church experiencing persecution to respond to an insult with a blessing (Eph 4:15; 1 Pet 3:9). In short, God cares not only that we resist injustice but how we do it.

DYNAMICS OF HIDDEN POWER

To this point we have been assuming that civil discourse is desirable and a necessary social virtue regardless of our views of the other side. But not everyone agrees. When civility concerns were being raised in the mid-nineties at a conference at Yale University, Benjamin DeMott wrote a powerful article decrying the call for civility. His concern was that civility was a tool of the leader-class to keep their "inferiors" in line, believing it was a form of silencing. He states, "The subject at Yale was the decline of civility, not of fairness, justice or decency among the privileged . . . the problem under consideration had to do with inferiors, not superiors; no tie was made between it and disrespect for the leader-classes stemming from thuggish leader-class beliefs and behavior."[9] He concludes his article with this simple statement: "When you are in an argument with a thug, there are things much more important than civility."

Clearly all do not agree that civility is an essential social virtue and a cure for our political ills. For DeMott, if the stew of society is full of rotten meat, there is no amount of the salt and pepper of civility that will make the stew wholesome. In fact, the salt and pepper is actually intended to do nothing more than to mask the flavor and keep the people eating the stew. In this case, civility is immoral, unloving, and needs to be harshly rejected.

The argument offered by DeMott and others like him actually acknowledges that civility can work when there is an approximate balance in power. When peers sit down at the table with one another, they should be civil and listen. They should seek mutual understanding and make mutual agreed-upon sacrifices and roughly comparable sacrifices. They can see eye to eye as persons even if they do not reach the same conclusions. However, when gross inequalities in power are present in society, civility takes on a very different character. The top dog and the bottom dog (to borrow language used in DeMott's article) can never see eye to eye, simply because one is on top and the other is on the bottom! They are not peers—perhaps they should be or we wish they were, but they aren't. In cases of extreme power inequity, civility can best be understood as a tool of the powerful to silence the disenfranchised. Therefore, the disenfranchised should not be bound by definitions and structures of civility created by the powerful, and they are free to resist if these definitions and structures are thrust upon them. In fact, they are obliged to resist. They may be accused of incivility, but, as DeMott puts it, this sort of incivility "needs to be recognized for what it is: a flat-out, justified rejection of the [power holder] claims to respect."[10]

A good example of rejecting of the claims of civility is found in an editorial by Michael Arceneaux. Arceneaux is a black journalist who admires President Obama in many ways, but he took issue with comments he made as part of the Nelson Mandela Annual Lecture:

> At the latter event, the former president asserted: "Democracy demands that we're able also to get inside the reality of people who are different than us. . . . Maybe we can change their minds, but maybe they'll change ours. And you can't do this if you just out of hand disregard what your opponents have to say from the start."
>
> I am never quite sure if Obama really thinks this naively or if he's trying to convince certain sects of the population— notably young black folks, whom he just loves to lecture—*that it's better to coddle white people about their prejudices with the hopes of growth rather than speak our minds as we see fit.*[11]

President Obama's call to civility is rejected, and in its stead is offered a call to "speak our minds as we see fit." Why? Because the sort of civil discourse that President Obama is advocating is, in reality, little more than coddling White people's prejudices. It is time to speak out against such prejudices instead of papering them over, this argument goes. The stew of society has rotten meat, and no culinary art of civility can make it palatable. What can be said in response?

IN DEFENSE OF CIVILITY

We take this objection to civility very seriously. Power imbalances are a real and problematic part of contemporary society, yet there's no doubt that some feel the extremity of power imbalance is not great enough to justify Arceneaux's argument. But let's take his point at face value and leave it to others to debate the magnitude, extent, and victims of power inequities. If Arceneaux is right about the inequities of our society, does the rejection of civility follow?

We think not. Let us offer some reasons why civility applies, even in cases where power is unequally distributed and effectively oppresses or disenfranchises groups of people.

The goal of civility is not to silence others but to help them be heard. One of the goals of the sorts of discussions we are advocating is to "achieve disagreement." In order to do this, we believe both parties need to understand the other, otherwise they have simply achieved misunderstanding, not an actual disagreement. The goal is for both parties to be heard—more than that, they have to be heard not just at a factual level but at an emotional level. We are advocating for empathy and being able to articulate the beliefs but also the feelings of one's opponents. This is certainly not silencing—either by intention or effect.

The problem with incivility is exactly what President Obama states—if you disregard what your opponents have to say from the start, they will be all the more likely to disregard what you have to say as well. Like begets like. Turning up the volume won't help. We can choose not to listen to each other; we can choose to speak in anger bordering on wrath. This works for those who are already on your side. You will be liked on Facebook and your talk radio show will receive high ratings, but unfortunately that simply produces more angry discourse from the other side. No one is heard but everyone is talking. This is the cycle we are hoping to break. Some may believe this is hopeless and that the other side is so far gone that shouting is the only appropriate response. Some may feel that giving one's opponents the basic respect of listening or sitting at the table with them is equivalent to validating their position. We disagree. Sitting and listening to someone does not validate their position; it simply respects their humanity—and just as importantly, it prods them to respect your humanity as well.

We do not offer civility as a replacement for advocacy. Arguments like those of DeMott and Arceneaux and other critics of civility suggest that civility solves nothing. At its best, civility only makes people feel better, but it does not offer a solution to our many vexing problems. Point taken. Nonetheless, changing the way people feel may be more important than we think. If by changing feelings civility contributes to mutual understanding and an improved communication climate, that is something important. It increases the likelihood that well-motivated people can work out real solutions to real problems. And it also increases the likelihood that they can keep working on the problem if their first attempt at a solution fails. Nuanced thinking is a natural product of empathetic listening to others who have differing viewpoints and is necessary to refine well-intentioned but ineffective policies—a phrase that probably describes most social policies when they are first implemented. Civility is not the solution to our social problems; it is just the precondition for being able to work together to solve our social problems. Civility does not do away with the need for advocacy; it simply makes it more likely that advocacy can actually build the sort of bridges necessary to move forward in the political realm with making effective policies and legislation, and to move forward in the social realm with reconciling longstanding animosities.

We won't make things better by swapping one hatred for another. The absence of civility makes it more likely that we will replace one form of hatred for another and one form of silencing for another. This may feel good or even just for those who have been long oppressed or long silenced. But inverse oppression is not liberation, nor is it a stable and healthy way to build a pluralistic society made up of diverse groups of people.

Consider the *Washington Post* editorial by Suzanna Walters with the provocative title, "Why Can't We Hate Men?" Walters, a professor at Northeastern University, is responding to the cascade of stories of sexual abuse that emerged from the #MeToo movement. It may feel like some sort of tipping point has been crossed, but she comments that for her, the tipping point had been reached long before, because male sexual misconduct is much older and deeper than just the recent events that have captured so much attention:

> Seen in this indisputably true context, it seems logical to hate men. I can't lie, I've always had a soft spot for the radical feminist smackdown, for naming the problem in no uncertain terms. I've rankled at the "but we don't hate men" protestations of generations of would-be feminists. . . . So men, if you really are #WithUs and would like us to not hate you for all the millennia of woe you have produced and benefited from, start with this: Lean out so we can actually just stand up without being beaten down. Pledge to vote for feminist women only. Don't run for office. Don't be in charge of anything. Step away from the power. We got this. And please know that your crocodile tears won't be wiped away by us anymore. We have every right to hate you.[12]

Walters is certainly making an important point that the events that spawned the #MeToo movement were not isolated exceptions but rather part of a pervasive pattern of powerful men using their position to exploit women. But as civil rights pioneer Howard Thurman notes, even when we have a right to hate, hatred is a dangerous and problematic choice. Thurman was one of Martin Luther King Jr.'s most influential mentors and one of the most influential advocates of nonviolent resistance. He was very deeply concerned that the sustained experience of injustice would make people give in to hatred. His thoughts merit quoting at length:

> In many analyses of hatred it is customary to apply it only to the attitude of the strong towards the weak. The general

impression is that many white people hate Negroes and then Negroes are merely the victims. Such an assumption is quite ridiculous. I was once seated in a Jim Crow car which extended across the highway at a railway station in Texas. Two Negro girls of about fourteen or fifteen sat behind me. One of them looked out of the window and said, "Look at those kids." She referred to two little white girls, who were skating towards the train. "Wouldn't it be funny if they fell and splattered their brains over the pavement!" I looked at them. Through what torture chamber had they come—torture chambers that had so attacked the grounds of humaneness in them that there was nothing capable of calling forth any appreciation or understanding of white persons? There was something that made me shiver.[13]

Thurman knew the reality of sustained injustice and oppression and was a tireless advocate for changing the structures and attitudes that kept this oppression in place. But he is equally determined to resist the temptation to give way to hatred and the sort of wrath described by DeYoung and denounced by the apostle Paul. In the story he tells, he does not assume the two teenage girls were born particularly hateful, but rather he assumes their unbridled hatred is a product of the "torture chamber" they have been through. Nonetheless, he is deeply disturbed by their inability to have any empathetic understanding of the life of a White person. Hatred cannot be solved with more hatred.

Stephen Carter, a law professor at Yale University, makes a similar observation in his book *Civility*. He comments on DeMott's article and acknowledges the real and often one-sided suffering that takes place in our society, but he advocates for civility nonetheless:

Therefore, when we ask others to choose to do justice, we may also be asking them to choose to sacrifice for the sake of justice. . . . Once more, the civil rights movement provides both the example and the truth: Civil dialogue requires us to sacrifice the opportunity to display our own self-righteous anger, even when we have good reason to be angry. It requires us to see God in those who would rather not see us at all.[14]

John Perkins, a renowned minister and civil rights activist, tells the story of his early years of ministry in Mendenhall, Mississippi. The problems of segregation and unjust laws were obvious, and he had expected them. However, he was leading a black church in the Jim Crow era, and the frustrations he found in working with his black congregants made him realize they had internalized the despair and were not willing to work on improving their situation. If they worked to change things, they were worried about what "the uptown people" would think. Perkins comments, "When I saw the twofold nature of the problem, I realized the solution—whatever it was—had to deal with both whites and blacks. Somehow whites and blacks would have to work together to lick this thing. And that was when I decided to try to get to know Reverend Robert Odenwald, the pastor of the First Baptist Church in Mendenhall."[15]

The story goes on to tell of some efforts at collaboration between Perkins and Odenwald and ultimately Reverend Odenwald's tragic suicide in response to the opposition he faced within his own congregation. Perkins follows up this story with a similar one about another White pastor he worked with who came to the same tragic ending.

Stories like this help us take the measure of the underlying problems we face. Saying, as Carter does, that "dialogue requires us to sacrifice the opportunity to display our own self-righteous anger," is not minimizing the depth of injustice, nor is it ignoring the power imbalances that often feed injustices. It is simply saying that giving in to hatred, refusing to listen to an opponent, being unwilling to cross the aisle, claiming to understand the other side while declaring they don't understand you, are all behaviors that will be returned in kind and no real progress will be made.

To refuse to listen is to refuse to love, and refusing to love is not an option. Much of the foregoing discussion applies to Christians and non-Christians alike. For Christians, however, the most powerful argument for civility is simply the absolute obligation we have to love others. We love our friends, we love our fellow believers, we love our family—these loves are commonplace. What is not commonplace is the Christian demand that we love our enemies and that we do good to those who persecute us.

In the course of the countless conversations that went into writing this book, we have been surprised and disappointed in the number of times people have simply suggested that there is no point in listening to "the other side." On the one hand, we've had conservative friends ask why they should listen to a social justice warrior who wants to replace evangelism with social policy. On the other hand, a different friend pointed out that one doesn't have to be very progressive to be extremely displeased with Mike Pence and believe that those who support him ought not to be given a platform. These friends are Christians, and the people they are referring to are also Christians. Each side may feel the other side is not particularly good or faithful in their Christianity. Perhaps they even feel that the other side is "ungodly." But nonetheless, Christians are to imitate the love of God himself which, as Paul notes in Romans 5, is a love that sent Christ to die for the ungodly. He goes on to note that "one will scarcely die for a righteous person—though perhaps for a good person one would dare even to die—but God shows his love for us in that while we were still sinners, Christ died for us" (Rom 5:7-8 ESV). So if God's model is to die for an ungodly person, in imitation of the love of God, is it too much to ask that we *listen* to an ungodly person?

CONCLUSION

This chapter has been casting a vision for conversations that rise above the river of our social circumstances rather than ones that just speed us downstream. Fighting the current of our social circumstances is not easy. To help us rise above, let's turn to Stephen Carter and Marilynne Robinson for some final words of wisdom.

Stephen Carter offers some insightful and provocative rules for civil discourse. These rules will not solve all of our social ills or eliminate power imbalances, either in the church or the broader society. But they contribute to an atmosphere that is more conducive to cooperative change and also more reflective of the love of Christ toward friend and enemy alike. Particularly relevant for our present concerns are these five rules:[16]

1. Our duty to be civil toward others does not depend on whether we like them or not.

2. We must come into the presence of our fellow human beings with a sense of awe and gratitude.

3. Civility requires that we listen to others with knowledge of the possibility that they are right and we are wrong.

4. Civility requires that we express ourselves in ways that demonstrate our respect for others.

5. Religions do their greatest service to civility when they preach not only love of neighbor but resistance to wrong.

Robinson renders Carter's rules (particularly rule #2) into an exceptionally helpful mental image that one can bring to a conversation with any person at all, but especially to an encounter with a person you might rather not be talking to at all:

This is an important thing, which I have told many people, and which my father told me, and which his father told him. When you encounter another person, when you have dealings with anyone at all, it is as if a question is being put to you. So you must think, What is the Lord asking of me in this moment, in this situation? If you confront insult or antagonism, your first impulse will be to respond in kind. But if you think, as it were, This is an emissary sent from the Lord, and some benefit is intended for me . . . you are free to act otherwise than as circumstances would seem to dictate. You are free to act by your own lights. You are freed at the same time of the impulse to hate or resent that person.[17]

We are free to act otherwise than what circumstances might dictate, as Robinson reminds us. The person from the "other side" who stands before you is an emissary from the Lord. Let us follow the road less traveled and choose to listen and to love even when all that is within us longs to shout and to hate.

10

HEALING JOINT PAIN
IN THE BODY OF CHRIST

I (Rick) still remember a breakfast I had over thirty years ago with a leader in our church. He was significantly older than I was, but more importantly, he was also wiser and more experienced. I often sought his wisdom when I was feeling angry or frustrated in my role as a pastor. This particular morning, I was frustrated with some chronic problems we were having with a ministry team, and I finally blurted out, "I don't mind having people problems; I hate it when people refuse to change!" My friend paused for a moment to be sure I was done blurting. Then he looked me in the eye and said, "Rick, some problems have to be managed rather than solved." After a brief pause, I said, "Yes, but I like solving problems better." And he said, "So do I, but some problems have to be managed rather than solved."

I didn't really enjoy that breakfast.

I went in with a problem and I came out with the same problem. Not exactly a flaming success. But on the other hand, I have gone back to this single sentence of advice time and time again over the past three decades: "Some problems have to be managed rather than solved." It has helped me have patience when problems seem intractable. It used to be if my efforts had not made the problem go away, I would despair and feel like I had failed. With this advice in mind, I have often realized that even if my efforts did not make the problem go away, they did help to keep the church together. It has helped me have hope. It has also prodded me to action when I have been tempted to avoid a problem—after all, the imperative is to *manage* the problem, and that is not the same as ignoring the problem or just living with the problem. Even if I conclude a particular problem cannot be solved, that does not mean it cannot be managed, moderated, or clarified. Just because two people disagree does not mean they have to go to war.

We live in the body of Christ. It is made up of many different members—hands and feet, eyes and ears, heads and toes. Each body part is connected to the others by a joint. Joints are subject to the Great Law of Joints: if joint, then joint pain. If you don't agree, you are under forty. Doctors say that there are 360 joints in the human body. 360 joints—that is basically one joint pain for every day of the year. Welcome to the life of a pastor!

To press the analogy, note that joint pain (particularly as we age) is a perfect example of a problem that has to be *managed*. I (Rick) am a runner—or at least I try to be. In recent years, I have been unable to run for extended periods of time because of knee pain, ankle pain, hip pain, back pain, and a pain in the arch of my foot. All joint pains occur at the conjunction of different bones or in the ligaments and tendons that hold the joints together. My daughter, a physical therapist, suggests that I do stretching and strengthening exercises. I do them. Usually the problem gets better. Then I quit doing the exercises because I think the problem has been solved. Then the problem comes back. As long as I manage the problem with stretching and strengthening, I can keep running. As soon as I think the problem has gone away and I quit stretching and strengthening, the problem comes back with a vengeance. My joints are fundamentally problematic, and therefore the best (and perhaps only) solution to my joint pain is simply to manage it well.

This book is really a book about joint pain in the body of Christ. It is a book about managing that pain in such a way that the body as a whole can continue to function well. And this chapter in particular offers management techniques. These techniques will not make tensions between different members of the body go away, but rather, they are designed to help the body of Christ keep functioning despite the fact that there are chronic pains. In effect, we are offering physical therapy instead of amputation as a solution to joint pain.

GOALS AND EXPECTATIONS

Having established that our goal is to manage conflicts successfully rather than solve them completely, let us offer a few hallmarks of a well-managed conflict. Specifically, let's identify three meaningful goals to pursue when we seek to bring together conflicting individuals or groups.

Goal 1: Achieve disagreement. Our first goal should be to achieve disagreement. Achieving disagreement may sound easy—"For heaven's sake, we achieved disagreement years ago! That's why we are fighting!" But in our experience, achieving a *misunderstanding* is much more common than achieving a real *disagreement.* Misunderstandings revolve around *perceived* disagreements, but the problem is that perceptions are often inaccurate. The easiest way to test the accuracy of a perception of a conflict is to ask a person to state the position of the other side. Frequently when people attempt to do this, they discover that the folks on the other side shake their heads and say, "But that's not really what I believe!" Here is a simple rule of thumb. Unless and until you can state the opinion of the other side in a way that makes them nod their heads and say, "Yes—you get it! You get me!" you have failed to achieve disagreement.

Stating the other side's position in a way that the other side finds agreeable always involves both facts and feelings. In other words, you need to be able to express what the other side believes but also how those beliefs make them feel and why those beliefs make them feel that way. For example, suppose John objects to using "Redskins" as a name for a football team. If Tina summarizes John's viewpoint as, "You think football teams shouldn't use stereotypes," she has almost certainly missed his point. Yes, John may object to stereotyping language, but much more is at stake for him. He feels using such language is further harming indigenous people who have already suffered from conquest, forced relocation, and organized efforts to eradicate their native cultures. Therefore, Tina would be much closer to the mark if she said, "You feel using names like this further alienates people who have already experienced horrible oppression. You don't want me to be politically correct; you want me to show some empathy!" This is much closer to capturing both the fact of the matter and the feelings that John brings to the table. Once Tina has stated it this way, there is a much better foundation for having a meaningful discussion. Conflicting convictions are almost never simply about propositional beliefs; they are almost always about the values and emotions. We don't achieve disagreement until the conflicting parties can clearly state what each other believes *and* why the matter is so important to them.

Goal 2: Achieve mutual respect. One of the most constant concerns of the New Testament is that we treat one another with respect—this seems to be particularly characteristic when addressing groups who might often find themselves contending with one another. When non-Christians ask us for an account of the hope within us, we are to offer it with gentleness and respect (1 Pet 3:15). We are to offer respect to whom respect is due and honor to whom honor is due, even if that person is a Roman ruler that persecutes Christians (Rom 13:7). We are to respect our leaders (1 Thess 5:12), our spouses (Eph 5:33), and our masters—and not just those who treat us well (1 Pet 2:18). Jesus famously modeled respect for others, particularly those who were disregarded, disrespected, or even despised by the prevailing culture: children (Mk 10:14), Samaritans (Lk 10:25-37; Jn 4:9), tax collectors (Lk 5:30), and Roman centurions (Mt 8:5-13). Particularly notable in the Gospel accounts is Jesus constantly extending respect to women in a culture where they were often silenced, disregarded, refused education, and where their word was regarded as unreliable testimony (Lk 8:1-3; 10:38-41; Mk 5:33-34; Jn 4:9, 27; 20: 16-17).

Simply put, we are to respect other people simply because they are people who are made in the image of God, people for whom Christ died, people who struggle with the same temptations as we do, and people who stand in as desperate need of a Savior as we do. In an ultimate sense, the things we have in common outweigh our differences. If we refuse to respect another human being, we are almost certainly laying ourselves open to be disrespected as well. Do we disrespect a person because they have dubious motives? Our motives are not pure either. Do we disrespect a person because they have sinned? We have sinned as well.

In any controversy, an essential quality to bring to the table is abiding respect for the others around that table. We need to be able to affirm their humanity and value them accordingly. We need to respect their rationality and therefore assume that a belief that we regard simply as irrational is probably a belief that we have simply misunderstood. Similarly, we need to see and be able to state how the actions of others have been guided by loving things that are good. Indeed, people almost always act for purposes that they perceive to be good and pursue courses of action that they believe to be loving. Their perceptions may be distorted, and their loves may be disordered, but when they tell the story of what they believe and why they believe it, they will almost never appeal to contradictions, evil intentions, and a desire to harm other human beings. Instead, they will appeal to good that you perceive to be good as well and offer arguments that follow the same logic that you use.

Goal 3: Identify and tend the common ground. Another reasonable goal is to identify common ground. Several aspects of the material we have presented in earlier chapters remind us that we have a lot in common. For example, the conviction spectrum begins with our common confessional beliefs and tends to reveal more and more areas we have in common before our differences actually emerge. Still more ways to find common ground will be discovered when we talk about conviction mapping in the following chapter. Honestly, our biggest problem is not the lack of common ground but rather our preoccupation with our differences—a preoccupation that makes us slow to acknowledge common ground and even slower to make something of it.

Common ground is like a plot of land. Once marked out, we decide what we will do with it. Let's assume we decide to plant a garden. In my (Rick's) experience as a homeowner, I have planted quite a few gardens. My wife and I are actually pretty good at it. We like clearing the land and tilling the soil. We like making planting beds and filling them with seeds or sprouted plants. We like making paths between the planting beds. During the initial rush of enthusiasm that comes when we first visualize the garden, it is easy for us to expend the energy needed to start the project. The problem is that the first weekend gives way to the rest of the week, and then the weeks give way to months, and the months turn into seasons. And somewhere in this progression (usually toward the beginning), our enthusiasm for the project wanes. We have other demands we must respond to, and new projects come up. Before long, the beautiful garden we joyfully imagined and dutifully planted gives way to weeds and bugs and rodents. By the time fall hits, the garden looks like any other neglected part of our backyard.

Common ground works the same way. Once people decide they actually want to communicate with those on the other side of a controversy, there is an initial enthusiasm. People will lean into the conversation and will do the exercises that are asked of them. Afterward, if the initial meetings go well, people can almost see the harmonious relationships blossoming in their midst. And then the initial weekend passes. First, we become busy with all the other things that demand our attention. In the midst of such busyness, we tend to only maintain contact with our friends—the other members of our in-group. It is not that we don't *want* to talk to the people on the other side, it is just that talking to them requires effort, whereas talking to our in-group happens by default. The common ground and provisional bridges are not intentionally dismantled; they are just neglected. Like a neglected garden, weeds aren't planted intentionally—they just grow on their own. Then funny things happen within your in-group. You forget the values and histories of the people on the other side of the controversy. As you talk about the issues, you drift back to old patterns. Someone in your in-group gives the perfect rebuttal of what you thought at the time was a good point made by the other group. If only you had thought of it at the time! Slowly your in-group begins to re-narrate the peacemaking efforts and rethink the foundations of all the bridges. At this point, you are not simply letting the weeds grow by neglect, you are actually fertilizing the weeds. Before long, the carefully identified and briefly tilled common ground looks more like a long-neglected vacant lot than a beautiful garden. The saddest moment in my own gardening experience is walking through the neglected garden late in the fall and seeing a shriveled vine that still has a single, withered tomato drooping on the ground. I can't help but think if I had just paid attention to the garden a month earlier, I would have had a whole harvest of beautiful, red tomatoes.

Common ground needs not only to be identified but also to be cultivated and tended. We need to remind ourselves of the shared values and beliefs we have by intentionally calling them to mind. We need to make the effort to maintain healthy relational contact with people on the other side. They do not have to replace our own in-group, but they cannot become aliens and exiles. And we need to be aware of our own self-talk. As I drive my car or mow my lawn, I often find my thoughts drawn to some of the controversies over convictions that I have a stake in. I am amazed and distressed at the thoughts that drift into my mind about the other side. I picture myself rehashing a previous conversation, exaggerating what was actually said, coming up with a perfect counterexample, calling to mind problematic experiences that cast doubt on the purity of motives of the other side. If I don't stop myself and intentionally call to mind the virtues, shared values, and common confessional beliefs that my opponents have, my self-talk will be fertilizing the weeds instead of cultivating the garden. If I do this, my only harvest will be withered and rotten tomatoes instead of the peaceful fruit of righteousness. Common ground must be tended.

CHARACTER NEEDED FOR CONTROVERSY RESOLUTION

As important as mutual respect and common ground are, character may be even more important. James is particularly eloquent on this point when he addresses disorderly conduct and quarrels. He appeals to his readers to be peacemakers using the "wisdom from above" that is "first pure, then peaceable, gentle, open to reason, full of mercy and good fruits, impartial and sincere" (Jas 3:17 ESV). Paul gives a similar exhortation in Romans 14:17-19, pleading for the church to not focus on issues of eating and drinking but rather righteousness and peace and joy in the Holy Spirit. Again, his confidence is that cultivating these character qualities will lead to peace and mutual upbuilding. Similar appeals to cultivating particular character qualities in the midst of conflict are found in many other writings of the New Testament (Gal 6:1; Eph 4:2; 1 Tim 6:11; 2 Tim 2:25).

Here is a quick overview of some Christian virtues that we should bring to the table when we seek to work for peace between conflicting groups:

Love. Love is the hallmark of Christian character and has a particularly important role to play in resolving conflict, but it is a concept that requires a bit of clarification. In American culture, love commonly means accepting someone and never judging them. It has no moral component. Viewed this way, love doesn't really shape our convictions but diffuses them—love is the wind that blows away the fog of our moral controversies and helps us embrace one another just as we are. But biblical love is quite different.

It has a direction—it always moves us toward the good and toward God. Love is a mighty river whose current pulls people toward God-appointed ends. That's why Jesus so strongly associates love with obedience. Our love for Christ is revealed by our willingness to obey him (Jn 14:15, 21, 23). God's commands point us toward God-appointed ends and good deeds. Jesus is our Lord and commander, and so in all matters our first concern is not pleasing ourselves but rather manifesting our love for Jesus by our obedience to his Word. Jesus-obeying love should infuse and shape our convictions, not diffuse and dismantle them.

Biblical love is also love for the church—for the body of Christ as a whole. We are called to a self-sacrificing love that is willing to limit our own personal expression of freedom for the sake of our brother or sister. If my brother or sister is grieved by what I eat, I am no longer walking in love (Rom 14:15). We are to be concerned with the interests of others above our own (Phil 2:4). If we have a complaint against a brother or sister, we should forgive them as Christ has forgiven us and then put on love that binds us together in perfect harmony (Col 3:12-13). We should submit to one another in light of our reverence for Christ (Eph 5:21). We should view those who are weaker as worthy of greater honor and never believe that we have no need of them but rather view them as indispensable because God has arranged it so in order that there might be no division (1 Cor 12:21-25). Paul himself sought to give no offense to Jews or to Greeks (referring to those outside the church) but also to give no offense to those within the church of God. In all cases he did not seek his own advantage but rather that of others (1 Cor 10:32- 33).

Passages like these and a multitude of others in the New Testament could not be more emphatic about the importance of preserving the unity of the body even at the expense of our own personal preferences and inclinations. When citing these verses, it is startling how quickly people respond by pointing out that these verses are used by some to keep people in abusive relationships. But the fact that these verses can be *abused* does not mean that they should not be *used*. Clearly the intent of these verses is *not* to create a safe space for abusers. However, they do have a proper and important usage and that is to restrain our natural (and culturally reinforced) inclination to be self-serving, demanding of all our rights, and resentful of any infringements on what we feel entitled to. We are certainly free to practice our Christian liberty. However, Paul is concerned about the times when we find ourselves face to face with a brother or sister in Christ who has a sensitive conscience—as much as possible, he wants us to avoid giving offense by declining to exercise our freedom and therefore easing tensions within the body of Christ.

One might also ask about the circumcision party, or those who deny the resurrection, or those who refuse to say Jesus is Lord—surely in these cases we may divide the body! In a sense yes, but biblically these issues are almost always presented as instances of people who are outside historical orthodoxy. They are not really a part of the body at all. In effect, we are called to discern the body but not divide it.

Finally, we need to extend love to the particular individuals with whom we have a controversy. Sometimes these are our weaker brothers and sisters, with whom we differ. In other cases these are people who have sinful motives. For example, Paul notes that some people are sharing Christ out of envy and rivalry, thinking to afflict Paul as he sits in prison (Phil 1:15). But Paul dismisses their attempts to afflict him and simply rejoices that Christ is being preached. Some people are just contentious—Paul wants us to flee from such controversies. If there are doctrinal errors, they are to be addressed but in a spirit of gentleness, hoping that God will lead them to a knowledge of the truth (2 Tim 2:23-25).

In short, a self-sacrificing love for Christ, for the body of Christ, and for the particular individuals with whom we disagree is the first prerequisite for dealing with Christian controversy. If love is not firmly in place, nothing good will follow.

Gentleness and humility. The New Testament describes quarreling using military language associated with battles and physical violence. Though this language is used metaphorically to describe the verbal contentions that are actually in view, it is a metaphor that describes the violent and angry attitude associated with quarreling. The defining feature of a quarrel is not simply that two parties disagree but that two parties disagree in an angry and wrathful manner. As a corrective to quarreling, the pastoral epistles focus on the *attitude* a leader is to bring to disagreements far more than it does to the content of disagreements themselves. The elder is to be gentle rather than violent (1 Tim 3:3). Similarly, Paul wants Titus to seek out elders who avoid quarreling and are gentle and courteous to all people (Titus 3:2). Even if a person is caught in a transgression, their correction should be marked by gentleness and humility—in this case the humble admission that any of us might fall prey to temptation (Gal 6:1). In the case of people who one fears have been "captured by [the devil] to do his will" (2 Tim 2:24-26 ESV), Paul's concern is that church leaders would avoid being quarrelsome but instead be kind to everyone and to correct opponents with gentleness (v. 25). In short, quarrels are associated with an attitude of anger or wrath, and the expectation is that spiritual correction will be offered with an attitude of gentleness and humility.

Gentleness and humility often travel together—indeed, these two qualities are the description that Jesus gives of his very own heart (Mt 11:29). They are the corrective he offers to our burdened hearts and the key to finding rest and living with a light burden. Indeed, pride overburdens us with a desire for control that is not rightly ours. As philosopher Rebecca DeYoung notes, pride leads us to false assumptions about who we are and the level of control that is rightly ours. Pride leads us to overstep our bounds and assert our will at the expense of others. This attitude of prideful control lurks at the bottom of Christian quarrels. DeYoung notes that gentleness offers a much-needed corrective: "Whereas wrath is rooted in pride, the strength of gentleness and the steadfastness of love in the face of adversity are rooted in a deep trust in God to handle things. How would our angry habits change if we focused more on God's justice and his control than our own claims and our ability to secure them against all threats?"[1]

Gentleness and humility point one toward God and remind us that he is actually in control, not we ourselves. As DeYoung goes on to say, "Humility is a virtue that keeps our claims on the world truthful and restrained. Humility and gentleness are twin powers against wrath, and both are rooted in love, a love that 'does not insist on its own way' (see 1 Cor. 13:4–7)."[2]

DeYoung is echoing a description of humility that C. S. Lewis offered many years earlier. He argues that humility is not thinking of oneself as lowly or worthless; it is much more like a self-forgetfulness. He suggests that if you were to meet a truly humble person, you would find him to be: "a cheerful, intelligent chap *who took a real interest in what you said to him*. . . . He will not be thinking about humility: he will not be thinking about himself at all."[3]

Gentleness and humility translate into people who are truly not preoccupied with themselves or even to their sides of the controversy. Instead, the humble person is genuinely concerned with the welfare of others. They would not call attention to perceived wrongs, refusing to say "Did you hear what they called me?" or "How can they question my integrity?" Their overriding concern would not be that "my side wins" but that Jesus is honored. As DeYoung puts it: "In wrath, we ultimately want our own way. In gentle self-mastery, we pray, 'Thy will be done.'"[4] This is the same quality called heavenly wisdom by James (3:17), a wisdom that is open to reason and peaceful, not always insisting upon its own rights.

A good illustration of the heavenly wisdom that is open to reason is found in the AND Campaign, founded by attorney and political strategist Jason Giboney. The movement encourages Christians to advocate for both biblical values and social justice. Their description of healthy activism includes a compelling statement about the significance of humility:

We believe humility is important, because politics and policy making are complicated, and the history of public policy is full of unintended consequences and misplaced priorities. We refuse to put the stamp of religious authority on prudential policy decisions. We hold convictions about what is best in our politics, but we hold these views with the understanding that we might be wrong. Politicians and others in politics should entertain that notion as well.[5]

This statement captures the balance between holding convictions deeply enough to boldly act upon them but at the same time humbly enough to still listen to others—not just out of ordinary respect but also because we humbly acknowledge the limits of our own understanding and know that we might be wrong. And humility also demands not just the possibility of intellectual mistakes but an honest acknowledgment of the possibility of our own moral failures. When convictions conflict, it is easy to feel self-righteous or judgmental about the people on the other side. We forget that there is much that could be judged about our own character. Marilynne Robinson, author of the Pulitzer Prize–winning novel *Gilead*, illustrates this well in her compelling description of an old photograph:

It shows a wild-haired, one-eyed, scrawny old fellow with a crooked beard, like a paintbrush left to dry with lacquer in it, staring down the camera as if it had accused him of something terrible very suddenly, and he is still thinking how to reply and keeping the question at bay with the sheer ferocity of that stare. *Of course there is guilt enough in the best life to account for a look like that.*[6]

Finally, it seems gentleness and humility are easily misinterpreted as a sign of weakness or timidity. Nothing could be further from the truth. Biblically, gentleness and humility are grounded in strength and confidence. It is exactly because we are confident in our beliefs that we do not need to be harsh in defending them. The case for truth is not made stronger by advocating for it with anger, wrath, or intimidation. Furthermore, the goal of addressing a quarrel is that others will come to the truth—that they will be persuaded. Anger and intimidation do not lead to persuasion but usually lead to fearful silence and withdrawal. As the saying goes: a man convinced against his will is of the same opinion still. We might create an apparent consensus by intimidating the opposition into silence, but it will not produce a united community striving side by side for the sake of the gospel.

Patience. Much that could be said of patience has already been covered in our discussion of gentleness and humility, but there is one more point that needs to be made. People change slowly, and patience creates time and space for us to grow. Thabiti Anyabwile, pastor of Anacostia River Church in Washington, DC, and a council member of The Gospel Coalition, makes this point as he reflected on the experience of his friend Nick. Nick wrote a blog post in 2016 strongly opposing the candidacy of Donald Trump. His post was met with a multitude of ungracious and vitriolic responses from fellow Christians. Vitriolic responses to a blog are common enough, but Anyabwile noted that his friend was "someone discipled *out of* the Democratic party *precisely because* he was taught and challenged about abortion. In other words, his story is the kind of story we conservative Evangelicals actually wish was more common."[7] But it seemed that many people felt that however far this person's theology had moved his political convictions, it wasn't far enough! Anyabwile goes on to say,

> We actually have so little tolerance for *political* disagreement . . . that we eliminate room and patience for the kinds of conversion and growth we hope to see. Our political vitriol becomes a barrier to our sanctification and that of others . . . to disciple well, people have to be able to think out loud, risk enough honesty to reveal their weaknesses, and receive patience from others so they can grow.[8]

It should be noted that Anyabwile himself is opposed to abortion, but he was also opposed to Donald Trump's candidacy. He would probably be one of the last people who would feel that Christian discipleship *requires* that one vote Republican, but he is simply pointing out that even if a person did feel this way, one must still allow others the time and space for discipleship to take place. Convictions neither form nor change overnight. We all need the space to think out loud, space that brothers and sisters in Christ grant each other by extending patience.

TROUBLESHOOTING OUR JOINT PAIN

Finally, just as there are things we naturally do that exacerbate joint pain in our physical body, there are also natural tendencies and habits that exacerbate joint pain in the body of Christ. An awareness of these tendencies can help us avoid them and thereby more effectively manage joint pain caused by our conflicting convictions.

Weaponizing. Weaponizing a belief was defined in an earlier chapter as taking a guideline for conduct, attaching it to a confessional belief, and then equating the two beliefs such a way that to challenge one is to challenge the other. The example given was equating gender roles with the doctrine of the Trinity. To be clear, connecting our beliefs about specific issues like gender roles to our higher (confessional) beliefs is actually something we recommend. It is an essential part of the spectrum of belief. But weaponizing is not simply making the connection, it is equating the two—as if the guideline for conduct *is* the confessional belief. To run with the analogy we have been using, this sort of weaponizing greatly increases "joint pain" and actually tends to justify amputations (excommunicating people from the body) rather than physical therapy (conflict management).

A second way we weaponize a belief is by "silver-bulleting." This means finding a particular verse that supports one's position and using it as a silver bullet that not only ends all conversation but also makes anyone who takes a contrary position into a person who denies the authority of Scripture. For example, we have heard entire discussions of the Christian faith and modern economics swept away by quoting the verse, "Thou shalt not steal." The implication drawn from the verse is that the government should not tax and redistribute money within an economy. Progressive income taxes that demand a greater percentage from the rich and distribute disproportional benefits to the poor are considered a violation of the command not to steal. Therefore, American free market capitalism is biblical (or would be with some further tax reform), and western European market systems are socialist and contrary to Scripture. But using the "silver bullet" blinds us to biblical passages that point in the opposite direction—for example, the obligation to leave corners of one's own field uncut so the poor can harvest them, or the canceling of debt in the year of Jubilee, or the mandatory tithe collected every third year to distribute to the poor and disenfranchised (Deut 14:28-29). Indeed, there are so many passages of Scripture that address the use and distribution of money, particularly in relation to poverty, that silver-bulleting an argument by using any single passage, no matter which way it points, is bound to oversimplify. It will also prove to be needlessly dismissive to well-intentioned Bible-centered arguments from the other side.

Flamethrowers. Flamethrowers are words and phrases that trigger anger and inflame the conversation, generating heat rather than light. They are commonly terms that are used lightly and freely by members of one's in-group. In fact, they are often a sort of shorthand for the beliefs of the other group. However, the members of the other group view those same words and phrases as judgmental, dismissive and inflammatory. They would also almost certainly refuse to acknowledge that the flamethrower words and phrases are actually descriptive of their group.

An interesting example of a flamethrower is the word *racist*. I (Rick) have been involved in a reading group that has made me aware of the radically different ways in which groups will use this term. A professor from another university was invited to campus to discuss diversity issues. One of her suggestions was to refer to ourselves as "recovering racists." Several people found this language to be inflammatory and irritating. Why should we assume that everyone is a racist? What have I done that indicated I'm racist? How can I claim to be a "recovering" racist if I don't believe I ever was one? Clearly, the term racist was a flamethrower for these members of our group. Others, in this case members of our group who were more "woke" and more sympathetic to social justice discourse, did not find this claim problematic at all when applied to the dominant group. In fact, for them, racism was largely a matter of institutional social structures that are developed along racial lines and used to favor one race over another. It was assumed that those who are members of the dominant group (in this case Whites) are racist, at least in some sense of the word.

At the moment, I am not concerned about who is right and wrong. Rather, the important thing is to understand that racist was a flamethrower word. Its use did not promote mutual understanding or a clearer perception of the issues at hand but rather tended to obscure the issues at hand and inflame the communication climate. This does *not* mean that the word should be censored or considered taboo. A healthy group can work through issues like this, and there may very well be a need for using such words, but one should use them with full awareness of the problematic effect they have for certain members of a group.

In the same group, there was a flamethrower that worked in the opposite direction: "neo-Marxism." It is not uncommon for more conservative thinkers to be suspicious of the contemporary social justice movement because they think it has been shaped by neo-Marxism, which interprets our social interaction largely through the lens of oppression. Equating social justice with neo-Marxism tends to be a flamethrower for the more progressive members of our group. They did not see themselves as neo-Marxists or any other sort of Marxist. And indeed, using that phrase in Christian circles seems to be a way of ending a conversation and dismissing a viewpoint without having to really consider it. Perhaps there was some truth behind the flow of intellectual history that was represented in this claim, but it felt far more like dropping a rhetorical bomb.

Using flamethrower words and phrases should be minimized or done carefully and with full knowledge of how one's opponents hear and understand the words. Otherwise, using these words only inflames the feelings of participants and makes the other side stop listening.

Fog machines. Fog machines are words and phrases that serve to confuse the participants in a conversation and obscure the issue that is really at stake. They are different than flamethrowers in that they do not necessarily inflame the conversation, but they are similar to flamethrowers in that they tend to stall the conversation rather than deepen it. They are also words or phrases that seem to work just fine within your in-group but are unhelpful when speaking to those who are outside of your group.

In fact, in the social justice reading group mentioned above, "neo-Marxism" would vacillate between being a flamethrower and being a fog machine. Once it was clarified that there was a real history involved in this statement and that it was not intended as a mere rhetorical bomb, a confusion emerged. What did this claim really mean? Who was the "Frankfurt School" (founders of neo-Marxism) and how could I be guilty of being one of them if I have never read them? Even after some explanation of the history and claims of neo-Marxism, it was very difficult for other group members to see how their opinions were really rooted in such a perspective. The claim was not so much inflammatory as it was confusing. It seemed to obscure the real issues that were at stake. It produced intellectual fog instead of dispersing it.

On the other hand, when people who were more involved in the social justice movement said, "Social justice *just is* the gospel," things got equally murky. They were using language that is not uncommon within their in-group. However, conservatives who are less attached to the social justice movement would never speak that way.

In fact, they were genuinely puzzled by what that claim could really mean. They did not think those who said this literally meant that believing in social justice saved someone from their sins and gave them eternal life, but salvation from sin and gaining eternal life seemed to be an essential part of the gospel to them. How could social justice *be* the gospel but not provide those things?

Again, the point of this story is not to argue any particular point about social justice. Rather, the point is to make all of us aware that the language we use within our in-group is often counterproductive when it is brought into a conversation with people on the other side of the issue. It may inflame the discussion (flamethrower), it may confuse the discussion (fog machine), but it almost certainly will not help the discussion!

Tripwires. Finally, it is always good to pay attention to what might be called tripwires. These are hot-button issues that may not correlate in a clear fashion to one's other convictions or opinions. In other words, one might stumble onto a tripwire in the midst of a conversation and suddenly discover that the entire communication climate has changed.

Peter Coleman, director of Columbia University's International Center for Cooperation and Conflict Resolution, tells the story of a friendly dinner gone bad for an elite research and development team at a top international consulting firm.[9] One of the members of the group was Jewish and had gone to Poland to participate in the March of the Living, a Holocaust remembrance event. One of the other members of the group was of Polish descent. Upon hearing the story of the March of the Living, he commented that always holding these events in Poland put an exaggerated level of blame on the Polish people. After all, the death camps were only built in Poland after it had been occupied by the Nazis! The Jewish member of the group was shocked and pointed out that large numbers of Poles were not only complicit but active participants in staffing these camps. Things escalated from there, and this highly effective working group was never effective again.

In this situation, all the group members were highly educated, shared liberal political convictions, and were all profoundly opposed to racism and Nazism. No one in the group was a Holocaust denier. There was no particular reason to think that simply answering the question "What did you do on your vacation?" would cause the group to implode—even if the answer happened to include a pilgrimage to Holocaust sites. But they stumbled over a tripwire—in this case, the way blame has been assigned to Poles for the Holocaust.

We have seen similar things happen within the church. A small group was discussing the importance of spiritual disciplines and one member suggested that the group should engage in sabbath-keeping activities. One of the group members reacted very strongly against this idea. In fact, they were upset that the group was discussing spiritual disciplines at all. It turned out that this group member came from a very traditional Seventh-day Adventist background and had grown up with extremely legalistic sabbath-keeping practices. The intense legalism and absence of grace had led them to abandon their Adventist heritage and every other form of Christianity for many years. They had only recently found the grace and liberation of a nonlegalistic faith and had absolutely no interest in returning to sabbath-keeping practices. For this group, sabbath keeping was a tripwire.

By definition tripwires are very difficult to anticipate ahead of time. However, once they have been discovered they must be addressed. Sympathetic listening and validation of the legitimacy of concerns that one may not feel personally can go a long way toward disarming these tripwires. It is never something to take lightly or dismiss with a cavalier suggestion to "just lighten up."

In conclusion, we hope this chapter has helped to clarify reasonable expectations to have as we enter into conversations about our conflicting convictions. The main point to remember is that these conflicts are like joint pain—they have to be managed rather than solved. Managing these conflicts can be a tedious task and also one that places profound demands on our character. It is said that the price of peace is eternal vigilance, and this is as true of war and peace between nations as it is between groups of fellow believers with conflicting convictions. We have abundant common ground with all who have a saving faith in Christ; the call to be peacemakers requires us to tend that ground with unwavering vigilance.

11

CONVICTION MAPPING

Should Christians vote for a presidential candidate *who is a known womanizer?*

Can I endorse a political candidate who is unabashedly pro-choice?

Is capitalism biblical?

Can a Christian organization use critical race theory to understand the plight of the marginalized?

Should a Christian university invite Muslim neighbors to come onto campus to jointly pray against hate crimes?

Is climate change really an important cause for Christian activism?

Sound familiar?

These questions and others like them have been batted around by students and faculty ever since we've been teaching at our university. Sometimes the conversations are cordial and productive, but increasingly they've been unproductive and ugly. We've gradually learned that the idea of getting everyone in a room and *talking it out* is deeply flawed. While leading a staff discussion concerning a controversial piece of art on campus, a man interrupted my (Tim's) introductory comments, stood up, and declared, "The moment that mural comes down, I leave the next day!" "Oh, brother!" someone in the front row whispered under his breath. You could feel the temperature in the room start to rise. What can we do when we find ourselves in situations like this?

To this point, we have considered why Christians have conflicting convictions and what the Bible teaches about these conflicts. We have suggested that there is a spectrum along which our theological convictions form. We have discussed both the importance of keeping the body of Christ together but also considered the reasons why Christians might need to part ways. In addition, we have considered some of the challenges of communicating convictions. In particular, we have noted the importance of the social context of our convictions and especially the role played by groups in developing and practicing our convictions. We have also considered some of the aspects of our personal history and how that affects the convictions we hold and the strength with which we hold them.

The time has now come to bring all these threads together and put them to work in order to build bridges and make peace in contentious situations. Though we will not offer a magic formula for resolving conflict, we would like to suggest a process that can improve the communication climate and broaden the opportunities for bridge building and peacemaking between individuals or groups that are experiencing the trauma of conflicting convictions. We call this process "conviction mapping."

CONVICTION MAPPING

The goal of conviction mapping is not to change convictions—either our own or someone else's. Neither is it intended to strengthen our own convictions if strengthening means providing better arguments to support them. Instead, conviction mapping helps us examine and understand our convictions, and it helps us to see how they are connected to our own life experience and to our social context and the groups of which we are a part. Conviction mapping also helps make us more aware of how our convictions emerge from our theological and confessional beliefs. In other words, this process *thickens* our convictions by helping us understand how deeply our convictions are woven into the fabric of our souls. Once we have done this, we are in a much better position to communicate our own convictions and also to listen to and understand the convictions of others. Thicker convictions also provide more points of contact with people who may not share our convictions, which in turn gives us more ways to build bridges and make peace.

The conviction mapping moves through five stages: clarifying our convictions, identifying the social context of our convictions, understanding the personal history of our convictions, "thickening" our convictions, and finally, understanding the convictions of others.

CLARIFYING OUR CONVICTIONS

Before conviction mapping can really begin, we must clarify what our convictions really are and why they are in conflict. In the previous chapter, we simply called this achieving disagreement. To develop this point a little further, notice that convictions are sometimes worded in ways that hide our points of disagreement, and this keeps us from talking about the real issues. For example, imagine your church is having a conflict over spiritual gifts and their place in worship services and small group meetings. Let's consider ways church members could state their convictions that might actually obscure the point of contention:

"I believe every Christian should experience the fullness of the Holy Spirit." This is a clear enough statement and sounds very reasonable, but it is so general that almost all parties would already agree with it. It offers no clue as to why a controversy is going on or what the controversy might be about.

"I believe every Christian can speak in tongues if they would like to." This is more specific, and every party to the controversy might not agree with the statement, but it only offers a belief that requires no particular course of action. It states something about the work of the Holy Spirit, but nothing about the way a church should be run, and the controversy is about how the church should be run!

"I believe every Christian must speak in tongues if they want to experience the fullness of the Holy Spirit in their lives." At this point, the controversial issues begin to emerge. This statement makes a claim about *all* Christians, and if it is true, a person cannot shun the gift of tongues without having their faithfulness as a disciple called into question. Nonetheless, there is no statement of any particular policies or practices the church should follow. We still don't really know what the disagreement is about.

"I believe our church's small groups should have regular times of speaking in tongues as a way to experience the work of the Spirit in our midst." At this point, an actual "guideline for conduct" has been identified. A particular practice is being recommended, and there are members of the church who would agree or disagree with this practice. This is a statement of conviction about a policy that is the source of disagreement.

The same progression could be constructed for people on the opposite side of the controversy. It might start with a general statement like, "The Spirit may work in different ways during different eras of the church." This sounds quite reasonable and easy to agree with, but it hides the controversy. A statement like, "I believe speaking in tongues should be forbidden in our church because the supernatural gifts ceased with the closing of the canon" is certainly less likely to sound congenial, but it makes the issue clear. The important point is that before we move ahead with conviction mapping, we must be able to state our conviction in a way that expresses our position on the issue that is actually being contested.

PERSONAL HISTORY OF OUR CONVICTIONS

Three years ago, the president of our university asked us to organize public conversations between faculty who disagreed on potentially explosive topics. Why not model for students how topics can be addressed without vitriol? We called these discussions "duologues," and our very first duologue came after the contentious

2016 election. We invited two faculty members—one a self-described progressive and the other a committed political conservative—to join us in the discussion.

While the event wasn't perfect, it went well and also served as a great learning experience. One of the most important things we learned was the value of advance preparation. Specifically, the invitation to our participants came with a stipulation—both would have to agree to dinner the week before the duologue. During this time, we guided them through a series of perspective-taking exercises asking them to examine their own personal beliefs, doctrinal convictions, and the other person's perspective. The experience was so valuable that we have repeated it for all the other duologues we have done. The most important exercise over dinner was to ask participants to give the backstory of their convictions. How did you arrive at your current convictions? Here's a quick outline of some of the questions we used to help everyone understand not only what each other's convictions were but also the personal story behind the convictions.

When did you first start to think this way? If you had to map out this conviction from its earliest beginning, where would you start? What influence did your family of origin play? Is it something your parents regularly discussed? How has your community influenced you? Just as Tim's community—consisting of mostly factory workers—played a key role in his positive view of unions, your community has equally shaped how you view people and situations.

What defining events, relationships, or life experiences crystalized your thinking about this issue? It is not only our family of origin and early life experience that shape our convictions. In a later duologue we addressed the question, Is capitalism biblical? In this discussion we invited five faculty to weigh in. As we had people tell their stories, we discovered that convictions were profoundly shaped by a life-threatening automobile accident, by relationships formed during a lengthy stay in South Africa during graduate school, and by a profound spiritual experience that made the person question the focus of his career. In some cases the life events were related to the issue of economics itself; in other cases the connection was quite indirect, but in all cases the experience profoundly shaped the person's convictions.

What emotions surface when you think about this issue? "You cannot stop having emotions any more than you can stop having thoughts," assert scholars from the Harvard Negotiation Project.[1] It's vital that we be able to articulate to ourselves and those within our group what emotions are driving our actions and activism. A few years ago, a rift happened within a church when older members felt marginalized by a push to recruit young families. In meetings they expressed *anger* at feeling left behind. When asked to be more specific in their description the older group came up with words such as *exasperated, offended, resentful, neglected,* and *chafed.* It was helpful to hear that they were not only angry but also felt deeply that they had been neglected, which in turn fostered a sense of resentment toward church leadership: *We've given our time, money, and heart establishing this church only to be cast aside.* The more specific we are in describing powerful feelings, the better we can identify the emotional element of our conviction.

SOCIAL CONTEXT OF OUR CONVICTIONS

Our convictions not only have a personal history but also a social context. More importantly, the *conflicts* we have over convictions are almost always deeply embedded in a social context made of groups of people, institutions we are a part of, and treasured histories and legacies that are passed from person to person and generation to generation. We cannot adequately understand conflicting convictions apart from their social contexts. Without us even knowing it, our social context can blind us to facts or numb us to the suffering of those from a different context.

One of the benefits of engaging others is that it can serve as a wake-up call. Getting an education in a predominantly White high school blinded me (Tim) to the deep racism inherent in our language choices and even what subjects were neglected, such as the Middle Passage—one of our nation's darkest hours where African families were ripped apart and sent to our shores. Here are some elements that help us identify the social context of controversies in which we may find ourselves:

What symbolic trigger prompted the controversy? In the rift between the older and younger members of the congregation mentioned above, strong emotions simmered for a long time without being acted upon. The tension remained below the surface until it was forced out by a "symbolic trigger," or in this case, two symbolic triggers. First, in order to make room for young families, the traditional service was moved from the main sanctuary to a smaller auditorium. One church member commented that it felt like being moved from the varsity field to a junior varsity field. Second, in order to give the main sanctuary a makeover, a silk screen was put up to cover the pipes of a massive and expensive pipe organ. To the older group this organ represented the tradition of the church that now was being hidden from sight. "When I look at that screen covering the organ it's like a middle finger being given to me every Sunday!" stated an exasperated woman. These "triggers" turned a breach into a crisis, resulting in the withholding of tithes, calling for an all-church meeting, seeking a change in leadership, and impassioned opinions being shared on social media.

Definition of the situation. Our social context, particularly the group(s) to which we belong, is usually the greatest influence that shapes our understanding of what is really at stake in a conflict. What is it that your group stands to gain or lose in this disagreement? Equally important is how you view what the *other* group is trying to accomplish. Last, what issues do both groups care about? In the scenario of the older generation feeling abandoned, the definition of the situation plays out as follows:

Beliefs about our group. The older generation is trying to protect the history of the church and make sure the scriptural command to honor the elderly is being followed (Lev 19:32; 1 Pet 5:5; Prov 19:20).

Beliefs about the other group: At best leadership is trying to recruit young families; at worst they are trying to force out the older generation.

What are we trying to do together?: A struggle is happening to define the identity of our church. Are we a contemporary congregation appealing to young families or a multigenerational church that honors and makes room for all generations?

Conviction mapping begins by clearly stating what our convictions really are but then sets these convictions within our personal histories and social contexts. The next step is to dive a bit deeper into the convictions themselves.

THICKENING OUR CONVICTIONS

Thickening our convictions actually begins with the backstory of our convictions, especially the personal history and social context of our conviction that we have just discussed. But it should be noted that our histories and group attachment do a lot more than just provide a context for our convictions; they shape our souls, form our affections, and guide our actions. Our convictions themselves are "thicker" than just beliefs that emerge from our theology or philosophy. To express this, we need to learn to put our conviction into a narrative rather than reduce it to just a rule, a reason, or a Bible verse.

Narrating our convictions. A helpful way to start narrating a conviction is to say something like, "Let me tell you what I think about immigration and why I think that I think it," or simply, "Here's what I think I think." Saying "what I think I think" is certainly saying an awkward phrase, and of course this wording is optional. However, it conveys some of the honest uncertainty that lies in understanding our own hearts and it also helps people to move into a storytelling mode rather than a teaching mode. In the teaching mode, we often just pass along propositional content instead of stories and experiences. It also tends to be a one-way conveying of information and arguments rather than an invitation to conversation. If we say, "Here's what I think I think," we invite others to say something like, "Yes, but have you thought about this?"

Narrating a conviction, then, begins with a clear statement of the conviction but then moves on to an informal, provisional telling of the story behind it. So, for example, if I (Rick) were to "narrate" my conviction about immigration, I might begin by saying something like this:

"Here's what I think about immigration. We need to open up our borders and become more welcoming to displaced people around the world. I believe this is an obligation we have based on the Old Testament teaching about sojourners and aliens in our midst, as well as because of New Testament teaching on loving our neighbor (a category that includes people of different ethnicity and even our enemies)."

This is a statement of my conviction and some specific support. Depending upon the particular immigration issue, I could add relevant specifics. Having stated my conviction, I could then tell some of the story behind it:

"Part of why I think that I think this is my own family history. My father was a first-generation immigrant who fled his home country when he was only fifteen. Several months earlier, his mother had been forcibly abducted from his home in the middle of the night and taken to a concentration camp. When my father fled his country, he had to leave his family behind. He never saw his mother again. He did not have a residency visa when he arrived in America, nor did he speak the language. Nonetheless, he was ultimately allowed to stay and finally became a citizen through serving in the army. My father was proud of America. When I think of his story, I am proud of America too. But I'm afraid America is losing a part of her soul—the part that for so long has welcomed the 'poor and huddled masses yearning to breathe free' as the Statue of Liberty inscription so aptly puts it."

This second part of my narration does not add a lot of information about exactly what we should do about immigration policy, nor does it add objective reasons for supporting a particular policy. However, if I were the other person about to engage in a discussion with me about immigration, I would sure like to know this part of my life story and the way it informs my convictions.

Tracing the spectrum of conviction. Convictions become thicker and better formed by tracing them across the spectrum of conviction described in chapter 2: confessional beliefs, moral mandates, core values, and finally, guidelines of conduct. The spectrum was given in this sequence because it is logical to move from the general principle to the specifics. Unfortunately, a sequence of logical reasoning is not always how we form our convictions. We think it is much more common for our moral reflection to begin with a moral intuition that is immediately felt, not produced by a step-by-step line of reasoning. We might call it the "voice of conscience." If our voice of conscience fits seamlessly within our moral community and general life experience, we may not even seek supporting reasons at all. We accept our moral judgment as sound and get on with our lives.

But sometimes life is rude.

Our comfortable moral intuition runs into life events or other people or even our own nagging doubts that call the intuition into question. At this point, we begin thinking about our moral judgment more deeply. We identify reasons why it might be true, usually reasons founded in our theological beliefs or deeply held morality. In effect, we are moving backward across the spectrum of conviction from a guideline of conduct (or perhaps a core value) that we intuitively held to find confessional beliefs and moral mandates congruent with our intuition. To be clear, we are not arguing that this is the proper way to form a conviction; it is just a way we commonly do it whether we are self-aware of that fact or not.

As life stirs the pot of our conviction, we not only have moments of personal reflection but also argue with others about our convictions. As a result of our reflections and discussions, we may refine or readjust our moral judgment; we may abandon it altogether; or, we may reinforce and deepen our moral judgment. As we have more experience, the process repeats itself. Conviction forming is not a simple linear process that moves from general principles to specific judgments. The process works like a spiral, moving around in a circular pattern that becomes tighter and tighter as it goes. As we continue to work the spiral, our convictions become thicker, more fully formed. This process is greatly aided by conversation with others—both those who agree with us and those who disagree.

We might think of a well-formed conviction like a callus. Repeated use of our hands for any given activity, whether playing a guitar or swinging a hammer, thickens our skin into a callus. The callus enables us to perform the task better and with less pain and for longer periods of time. Likewise, a conviction that is regularly expressed, examined, and questioned becomes thicker. It becomes more durable and less likely to be hurt. And when our convictions are more durable and less likely to be hurt, they are easier to talk about, especially with those who might disagree. On the other hand, thickening our convictions may actually help us rethink our convictions. It helps us bring up hidden reasons for why we feel the way we feel. Those reasons may be sound, but sometimes they are really just byproducts of our upbringing or prejudices common to the groups of which we are a part. Either way, thickening our convictions is the best starting point for peacemaking and bridge-building conversations.

Core values. One particularly valuable part of tracing out convictions across the spectrum is that it helps us think more directly about a neglected part of the conviction spectrum: our core values. As was stated in chapter three, we are using the phrase "core values" to describe values that are universally shared (or shared among all Christians, in the case of Christian values) but differently prioritized. It helps a lot to explain to others exactly what core values are motivating our actions and how we weigh those values in comparison with other values that might apply.

To give an example of this, let's consider the core values that might be hidden in the conflict about the use of spiritual gifts mentioned earlier. What happens when we share values but weigh them differently? One person might place a high value on the expression and experience of supernatural power. They are worried that we too often hold to the form of religion but deny the power of it. Therefore, they are advocating for free and bold usage of the supernatural gifts. A second person agrees that experiencing the supernatural is important, but they are profoundly concerned with the unity of the body of Christ and are quite willing to sacrifice personal freedom of expression for the sake of preserving relationships within the church. When a gift is valued too highly above others, it makes those who possess other gifts feel devalued—like they are second-class citizens. A third person also values unity but strongly feels that unity cannot be purchased at the price of theological integrity. The things spoken in tongues often go uninterpreted, and even when they are interpreted, the interpretation cannot readily be checked or verified as coming from God the way that Scripture can. Finally, a fourth person may agree with all the values that have been identified by others but feels that none of these is as important as the testimony of the church to the nonbelieving world. They want to be sure that if nonbelievers come to church, they understand what is being said and can potentially be convicted by the Spirit. Outbursts of people speaking in an unintelligible language would just seem chaotic rather than convicting.

All of these values are legitimate—in fact, they can all be grounded in Scripture; presumably all Christians should share these values. However, they produce very different and perhaps incompatible guidelines for conduct because of the different ways the values are weighted. If one wants to build bridges between these groups, identifying the relevant values may be important. It may be possible to manage concerns about outsiders by diligently requiring interpretations to be given as well. This might help build a bridge between a person who wants to have supernatural manifestations of the gifts and a person who wants worship to be accessible and convicting to outsiders. On the other hand, it may not address the concerns of a person who is worried about devaluing others and creating second-class disciples. The important thing is to understand the motivating values that underlie our position in order to help identify what sorts of bridges can be built.

UNDERSTANDING THE CONVICTIONS OF OTHERS

A Baptist once said to an Episcopalian, "I can't hear you because of what I think you're going to say!" When you think of the group you find yourself at odds with, what do you expect them to say during a discussion? How accurate is your assessment? A final step of mapping our *own* convictions is trying to understand the convictions of *others*.

Categories and characteristics. As you think about members of a different group, what categories do you put them in (e.g., liberal, ultraconservative, progressive, pro-union, pro-administration, egalitarian, complementarian)? What emotions do you attach to the category you've placed them in? For example, when you think of "egalitarian"—believing that men and women are equal in all leadership roles—does it cause anger to feel that Scripture is being disregarded for the sake of pleasing our culture? Does the term "conservative" cause you to shake your head at people you think are being blindly guided by old models or traditions? The danger with putting people into rigid categories is that it makes it so easy to completely dismiss them.

Today, a generational feud has surfaced between boomers and Gen Z. Twenty-five-year-old representative Chloe Swarbrick was giving a floor speech in the New Zealand parliament. When an older political opponent shouted out an objection, he was met with, "OK, boomer."[2] The video went viral and Gen Z had the perfect dismissive response. Once put into the category of boomer, any objection or critique is summarily set aside. While categories can help us group and identify people, we must not allow them to become defensive devices that allow us to ignore others.

Correction. When considering other groups, how balanced are you in your view of them? An exercise we often use to help balance our thinking of the opposing group is to write down three negative and positive qualities you associate with them. For example, if you think of those in the other group as "liberal," you may characterize liberals as (1) caring more about social issues than biblical concerns, (2) being naive about the Marxist roots of social justice, and (3) neglecting evangelism to meet merely physical needs. To balance this out, you may acknowledge that liberals (1) actively care for the homeless, (2) obey sections of the Bible that command us to care for physical needs, and (3) generously give of their time and money. Recognizing positive qualities does not eliminate the negative concerns, but it does broaden our view and add complexity to oversimplified stereotypes.

Acknowledging the good qualities in others can become a mental habit that psychologists call "positive recall bias." In one study participants were divided into two groups and given simple instructions: one group was asked to write down five things a day for which they were thankful; the other group was to write down five things they would identify as a hassle or disappointment. Each group did this for ten weeks. The group seeking to cultivate a positive recall bias reported that over time they became attuned to notice the good—both in people and situations. Conversely, the negative recall bias group grew much more attentive to what they didn't like in people or situations.[3]

Simply put, we train ourselves to either recall good or bad things about a person. Over the past decade, Justin Brierly, a Christian apologist and radio personality in the United Kingdom, has interviewed hundreds of atheists. You would think he'd be pretty jaded toward people who criticize our faith. Not true.

It reminded me that there's a real danger of Christians (myself included) caricaturing atheists as sneering, cold-hearted haters of religion. I'm sure some of those exist, especially online, but in person, atheists rarely conform to that image. Brown [well-known British atheist] is that kind of person I'd like to share a drink with down at the pub, as are most non-believers I know. In many respects, we like, love and laugh in the same way as each other. We just disagree about the basic nature of reality.[4]

Brierly has had the chance to engage one of today's most notorious atheists, Richard Dawkins. We might think he would be hard pressed to think of anything positive about such an outspoken and often mean-spirited opponent of our faith, but that is not the case. "Despite his anti-theism, I have a lot of affection for Richard Dawkins." Why? Dawkins's spirited opposition to the faith has made Christians "up their game and think through their faith more critically."[5] More than anything, Brierly is thankful to Dawkins for forcing the God question back into the public arena and "revitalizing a Christian response through apologetics in the Church."[6] If Brierly has developed a positive recall bias toward atheists, surely we can do the same for fellow Christians who don't share our own convictions. Yes, we may disagree on how to interpret certain biblical passages or how to best reach out to young families in our communities, but we share a common commitment to do what the Scriptures advocate and to minister to the upcoming generation. By the Spirit's help, let us cultivate a positive recall bias to see the good first, then focus on our differences.

Engaging in perspective taking. While it's understandable to focus on your group's position and supporting arguments, we should also be familiar with the best arguments for the other side. If you had to argue for the other group's position, what would be the very best case you could make? What biblical support do they subscribe to? What books or experts do they quote? After learning their perspective, how might you even make their case stronger?

While in graduate school, I (Tim) had a professor who provocatively argued that gangsta rap music—filled with cursing, dehumanizing views of women and gays, and rampant sex—ought to be viewed as a resistance movement against racist White dominant culture and should not be censored. He traveled the country debating those who disagreed with him—which were many! He impressed our class by giving the perspective of those whom he debated and even strengthening their argument against him. "I would have said to me . . ." was a constant refrain he used. Couldn't we do the same for our opponents within the church? Could we go the extra mile and not only know their best arguments but take time to strengthen them? After your group has studied the perspectives of others, ask yourself where you *agree?* One of the telltale signs of bias is to view another group as being totally wrong on *every* issue.

Finding middle ground. To help your group discover middle ground, ask: "What changes to the other group's argument/position would make it (more) acceptable?" For example, perhaps your group would support a leadership decision to pursue young families *if* a traditional service tailored for older congregants would be protected and fully resourced (e.g., in the main sanctuary, with a full orchestra, singing traditional hymns). If you are asking other groups to compromise, what compromises are *you* willing to make? And, is your middle way really a compromise or skewed in one direction? Last, what one demand on your part would destroy the compromise relative to the other side? For example, demanding *all* services at your church should be traditional leaves no room for preferences of a younger generation.

Groupthink. As already suggested, groups can be a huge asset (inviting members to discuss issues) or a liability (discouraging any form of dissent). How well does your group allow differing perspectives within the group? Is the highest value of the group uniformity? Do members feel the freedom to disagree with the direction the group seems to be heading in? Does in fact the group leader invite dissent?

Inviting outside perspectives. How often does your group invite outsiders to challenge your perspective? If outsiders do come in, how are they treated? Does leadership seek to cultivate common ground with the outside speaker, or is the exchange combative? How committed is your group to the relational level of communication (acknowledgment, respect, compassion) when engaging outsiders? When outsiders present their case, is your group good at listening, or do people interrupt and dominate the conversation? "To answer before listening—that is folly and shame" (Prov 18:13). Proverbs attaches shame to those who don't listen. However, the inverse is surely true—listening to a person before speaking is to confer honor.

Goodwill of the group. When facing disagreements with other groups is your inclination to seek divisions or fences? How does your group talk about others? In writing to the church at Colossae, Paul reminds them that prior to conversion while living among nonbelievers they "used to walk" in their ways. But now, "you must also rid yourselves of all such things as these: anger, rage, malice, slander, and filthy language from your lips" (Col 3:7-8). Last, how quickly does your group seek to weaponize—making it an intractable position that must be adopted by all—your group's particular position?

CONCLUSION

There is great danger in isolating ourselves in communities of like-minded people. If we don't talk to those who disagree with us, we become sure of our opinions but also more narrow and more extreme in our thinking.[7] According to the Atlantic 2019 Pluralism Survey, nearly 40 percent of Americans interact with a person from a different political party only a few times a year or never. In short, for all Americans' talk about diversity, we like sameness a whole lot more—especially when it comes to thinking.[8]

Surely followers of Jesus can do better in conversing among ourselves. The early Christian movement was comprised of an unlikely assortment of Jews, Gentiles, women, men, rich, poor, and the most neglected group of all—children. They were all equal at the foot of the cross, and their differences in backgrounds and perspectives eventually became a strength and not a weakness. No doubt coming together entailed many conversations filled with tension and compromise—just read the New Testament epistles. The first step in coming together is to map and understand our own convictions. "The purposes of a person's heart are deep waters, but one who has insight draws them out" (Prov 20:5). By first examining our own hearts and mapping our convictions can we begin to understand the deep waters of the conviction of others.

12

GUIDELINES FOR HARD CONVERSATIONS

We have covered a lot of territory in this book. There is probably more here than anyone can keep in mind as they walk into an actual conversation between individuals or groups with conflicting convictions. Therefore, we'd like to offer some guidelines for those who are willing to engage in hard discussions—phrases that are easy to remember but capture some of the most important attitudes and strategies to bring to peacemaking conversations.

FENCES MAKE BETTER PLAYGROUNDS

All the rest of our slogans will deal with disputable matters and personal convictions, but we must start with our absolutes. The most important thing about our absolutes—our defining confessional beliefs and moral mandates—is that they be clearly identified and well-tended.

Some landscape architects did a study comparing playgrounds surrounded by a fence to comparable playgrounds without a fence. The difference was striking. On playgrounds without fences, the children tended to gather around the teacher and were reluctant to stray far from her view. They felt unsafe, and much of the playground went unused. On playgrounds that were fenced in, however, they ran all around the entire playground, feeling more free to explore and engage in unstructured and creative play.[1] Good boundaries make for better playgrounds, more creativity, and better self-expression.

We have discovered that the same is true for convictions. In order to have the freedom to explore and express differing Christian convictions, we need to have the confidence that our defining confessional beliefs are being protected. This is the value of doctrinal statements, confessions of faith, and the like. They serve as fences. If they are in place and well-tended, we are free to roam. If there is no fence, or if the fence is not well-tended or clearly visible, we feel unsure and less able to explore. Therefore, the first thing we want to be clear about is the need to recognize and tend our boundary commitments and defining beliefs. A community with clear and well-tended defining beliefs is free to express those beliefs in a wide variety of ways.

DIFFERENT CONVICTIONS ARE A FEATURE, NOT A BUG

It is uncanny how often people complain about the behavior of an app or computer program—claiming it has an irritating "bug." But oftentimes the irritating *bug* is actually a valuable *feature* that the user just doesn't understand. Since they don't understand, they complain about it instead of putting it to good use. The same is true of differing convictions in the body of Christ. They are a feature not a bug.

Jesus designed differences into his body. They serve a positive purpose and should be valued and respected. As a pastor, I (Rick) was always struck by how much of what actually got done within our church was done by members who thought their particular ministry was the most important thing in the world. For example, we had a wonderful recovery ministry. It was led by a couple who were zealously committed to working the twelve steps because it literally transformed their Christian walk. They wanted others to join a recovery group. In fact, they wanted *everyone* to join a recovery group because we are all addicted to sin. We had another couple who were zealously committed to disability ministry—not because disabled persons had so many needs but because they had so much to offer. They wanted disabled persons to be part of everything, and they wanted everyone to be a part of the disability ministry! They advocated for disabled persons to serve on the worship team on Sunday morning, to care for our children, to be our ushers and greeters; they recruited small groups and high school students to help with events. I had similar ministry advocates for every effective ministry in the church. These ministry advocates were incredibly diverse in their passions and convictions. The only thing they shared in common was the belief that their ministry was the most important in the world. And, they tended to have thriving ministries. The ministries that didn't thrive usually had leaders who lacked this sort of zealous conviction.

I realized differing convictions were a feature, not a bug. I became a fan of different convictions, zealously expressed and passionately pursued. It got things done. Everybody was passionately building on the foundation that Christ had laid, and as long as we didn't burn each other's buildings down, we could make a thriving community. If each ministry leader respected the overall church leadership and was willing to accept the fact that everyone else wasn't quite as excited as they were, things worked great.

CONVICTIONS ARE LIKE STEAKS: THE THICKER THE BETTER

As we have clearly stated in this book, convictions are thick in the sense that they are a lot more than just a belief or a fact. If we are sharing our convictions with someone else, we should be thinking of telling them a story, not staking out our position. Like showing one's work on a math problem: you can get partial credit even if the grader believes the answer is wrong. It helps a lot to have something we can share that those on the other side can understand

and appreciate. Convictions emerge from our life stories, express our life passions, and inform our dreams. We can talk to each other about these things and feel respected, understood, and appreciated. Even if it doesn't lead to agreement, it's less likely to lead to an argument.

BE A CHIMP, NOT A RHINO

If someone else's convictions don't make sense, it's probably because you don't understand either their backstory or the conviction itself. Your first goal is to understand. That means you need to be a chimp, not a rhino. Rhinoceroses are notoriously shortsighted—it is said they can't tell the difference between a tree and a human being from fifty feet away. And that explains their aggressive behavior. If they don't recognize it, they ram it; it's hard on both the trees and the humans. It isn't even that great for the rhino. It's bad news all around. Chimps are different. When chimps see something they don't recognize, they go investigate. They pick it up and prod it and play with it. They try it on their heads to see if it will fit. If they decide it's not for them, they set it down and pick up something else, but at least everybody has had a good time and can walk away without being rammed. If your brother or sister in Christ has a personal conviction you don't understand, be curious, investigate, and ask questions that you really are interested in getting the answer to. Don't ram them. Be a chimp, not a rhino.

I NEED TO ALTAR MY CONVICTIONS

Yes, notice the spelling. My conviction is first and foremost an act of devotion—something I put on the altar. I do it for Jesus, and communicating it to others is a secondary issue. My convictions help me make my life a living sacrifice to Jesus. Convictions put shoe leather on the claim that we are bondservants to Jesus our Lord. It is fine and often helpful to talk with others about our convictions. And it is in the nature of talking about things that we sometimes change our minds or the minds of others. One might call this altering one's convictions or altering the convictions of others. We are simply suggesting that this sort of altering is not our primary responsibility toward others in disputable matters. Normally, we should be happy to let others bring their convictions to Jesus just as we bring ours. More "altaring," less altering.

MAKE YOUR CHURCH AN ART GALLERY, NOT A COUNTY FAIR

Though I do enjoy going to county fairs, I have noticed that everywhere you look there is another ribbon. Blue, red, and white—first, second, and third place; occasionally a yellow ribbon for honorable mention. Everything is "entered" at the county fair, and everything is judged. There are more ribbons than flies. In an art gallery, things are just there to be seen and admired. Sometimes they are labeled, sometimes they are explained, but they almost never have a ribbon. There is no award for "Best Painting of a Beach." It would be nice if our convictions could be more like the art gallery—that they could simply be shown in public and others come and admire what they see. They may talk about our work, they may critique, or they may give us good ideas. But this is all best done as conversation rather than judgment. At the end of the meeting, no ribbon need be given for "Best Conviction Concerning Tax Cuts."

REPORT UNATTENDED BAGGAGE

An unaddressed point of contention it is often called "the elephant in the room." These elephants tend to be seen by everyone and nurtured and fed by our groups. It is good to identify them and talk them out. What is much trickier is unattended baggage. These are issues that are easy to miss—they are the opposite of elephants. These issues are nourished by individuals rather than groups as a whole. Members of an in-group all tend the same elephant, but they may very well have completely different baggage.

Baggage is okay—we expect people to bring baggage on a peace-making journey. It's the unattended baggage that you have to worry about. It doesn't look like much, but it might hide a bomb. The indicator is usually a person who is being too quiet. Perhaps the person is nursing a grudge; perhaps the person has a question that they are afraid to ask for fear of sounding like a heretic—or perhaps they fear sounding like a witch hunter; perhaps it is a person with a hurt they are afraid to bring up. Whatever the issue, and whomever the person, all of us have the responsibility to keep our eyes open for unattended baggage in the room. We need to be willing to gently and lovingly ask if we are missing something. And just like actual unattended baggage, not every piece of it hides a bomb. Sometimes baggage is just forgotten, and the reminder to tend it is very welcome. Sometimes a person is just naturally quiet and not prone to share but is fully engaged in what is going on. But if you are trying to resolve a conflict and you see someone who is disengaged or sense that an issue is unaddressed, it's your responsibility to report the unattended baggage.

These are our final tips. We pray you will find these helpful as you engage in peacemaking and bridge building with those who see things differently than you do. May you walk in the wisdom from above that is "first pure, then peaceable, gentle, open to reason, full of mercy and good fruits, impartial and sincere. And a harvest of righteousness is sown in peace by those who make peace" (Jas 3:17-18 ESV).

13

HISTORICAL POSTLUDE

CONVICTIONS IN NAZI GERMANY

Few of us would recognize the name of Pastor Paul Schneider. It is a name I (Rick) first encountered staring into a pale green cell while visiting the Buchenwald concentration camp. I was surprised to see a bouquet of flowers set beside a plaque on the back wall of the cramped cell. It identified the cell as the one which Paul Schneider, the "Preacher of Buchenwald," had occupied before his death. I have a personal interest in the Nazi era, and I was fairly familiar with many prominent figures of the church in and around this time. Schneider's name, however, had never come to my attention. A little research led me to discover one of the most remarkable yet unknown martyrs of the twentieth-century West.

Schneider was appointed to pastor a small Reformed congregation in Germany during the mid-1920s and continued in this capacity for almost a decade, pressing his congregants to take the Bible and the catechism more seriously and faithfully modeling complete devotion to Christ. In 1933, when Adolf Hitler came to power, Schneider's deep Christian convictions immediately brought him into conflict with the Nazi regime. He refused to ring the church bell to signal the beginning of Nazi meetings. He refused to return the Nazi salute. When the German Christian movement, which supported the Nazi cause, began to exert leadership within his denomination, he withdrew and became affiliated with the Confessing Church—an organization of churches that opposed Hitler. He went through a cycle of arrests and persecutions at the hand of the Nazi leadership. Finally, he was arrested, fined, and offered a conditional release if he was willing to accept banishment from his current pastorate. Schneider refused because he believed the government had no authority over the relationship between a shepherd and his flock. In November of 1937, he was incarcerated in the infamous Buchenwald concentration camp. His martyrdom was recorded by a clerk who served in the camp:

> In the spring of 1938, there was an order that all prisoners passing by the Nazi flag on their march to work should greet it by taking off their caps. Schneider declared that this saluting of the Nazi flag was idolatry and he refused to obey the order. . . . He was called to the SS and freely confessed his attitude. . . . Schneider received in his body repeated and heavy tortures, humiliations and pains. All the ingenuity of Nazi sadism was used against him. Torture was alternated with good treatment and appeals to relax his strong opposition. Schneider was unmoved. . . . The worst time for Schneider was in the early summer of 1939. For several days he was hung up, with his hands behind him and his body permanently bent. This devilish device caused him continuous pain. His suffering was borne nobly and he was greatly honored in the camp.[1]

Schneider died about a month after this final torture. His wife, Margarete, claimed the body, and he was buried in the graveyard of one of the churches he had faithfully served. The site became a source of inspiration and consolation to many who were to follow him on the path of persecution.

What is most important for the purposes of this book was the nature of his personal convictions. As he understood the call of the gospel upon his life, he felt that he dare not make any accommodations to the Nazi regime at all. He refused to ring the church bells, he refused to make the Nazi salute, he refused to remove his cap for the Nazi flag. The result was an early death—indeed, his death took place before WWII had even begun. His convictions were strong, clear, deeply held, and absolutely unwavering even in the face of physical torture. Obviously, Pastor Schneider was more faithful to his convictions than countless other Christians of the Nazi era.

Consider, for example, the conduct of another pastor about a year later. By this time, WWII was in full swing. Germany had invaded Poland in September of 1939, and in spring of 1940, they conquered Holland and Belgium. On June 14, 1940, the Nazi forces entered Paris. As it turned out, two pastors of the Nazi-opposing Confessing Church were visiting a church in eastern Prussia that day. It was a beautiful afternoon, so the pastors rode a ferry across to the town of Memel and were enjoying a meal at an outdoor café. Suddenly, the quiet afternoon was shattered by a trumpet fanfare declaring France had surrendered! A pandemonium of Nazi fervor erupted. Some people leaped onto chairs and tables and began singing "Deutschland über Alles" and then the "Horst Wessel Song." All around the pastors, café goers were rising to their feet, throwing out their arms in front of themselves and offering the "Heil Hitler" salute. Imagine the shock when one of our two pastors turned toward his friend and found that he had jumped up and offered the salute as well! As his friend looked on in stunned silence, the pastor leaned down to him and said "Are you crazy? Raise your arm! We'll have to run risks for many different things, but this silly salute is not one of them!"

What should we make of this gesture? The pastor was a member of the Confessing Church, which was organized to oppose Hitler. Had he flipped sides now that Hitler was having some success? Had the pastor gone mad? Was he a coward? A traitor? I told this story to a class of university students, and they were unanimous in their condemnation of this pastor and could not even imagine circumstances under which such behavior would be permissible.

Imagine the gasps and stunned silence when I told them that the pastor offering the Hitler salute was none other than Dietrich Bonhoeffer.

Bonhoeffer's behavior is startling on many levels. On the surface, it surely seems either cowardly or hypocritical. It is clearly the exact opposite of Paul Schneider's response. Schneider had steadfastly refused to offer the Nazi salute since the earliest days of Hitler's rise to power. When questioned by the SS, his explanation was simple: "I cannot salute this criminal symbol." Bonhoeffer, on the other hand, simply saluted—no threat or coercion required! He even encouraged his friend to join him in the salute!

Understanding the dramatic difference between these two Nazi martyrs is made much easier by the analysis of convictions that has formed the backbone of this book. Their differences offer a perfect illustration of the spectrum of convictions as well as some of the other tools we have suggested for dealing with Christian conflicts.

First, let's thicken Bonhoeffer's convictions with an account of his personal history. Bonhoeffer, like Schneider, opposed Hitler and the Nazis from the earliest days of their rise to power. In 1933, a radio address he was giving just a few weeks after Hitler took power was cut off midsentence—the Nazis were listening and found his position profoundly at odds with their own, so they shut down the broadcast. Bonhoeffer participated in founding the Confessing Church in 1934, the organization which Schneider joined, and in 1935 he was instrumental in starting an underground seminary in Finkenwalde that served the Confessing Church until the Gestapo closed it in 1937. His opposition to the Nazi regime was so transparent that many of his friends feared for his safety and implored him to go off to America in June of 1939. Bonhoeffer did so but soon regretted his decision and returned to Germany because he felt he could not participate in rebuilding the country if he fled during its darkest hour. He decided to return and face whatever might befall him during the course of Germany's worst period.

Clearly, Schneider and Bonhoeffer shared a deep disdain for the Nazi regime—a disdain born of their shared Christian convictions. However, some reasons for their differences emerge as we consider the backstory—particularly Bonhoeffer's family. He came from the German aristocracy, and his family was exceptionally accomplished. His father was the most renowned psychiatrist in Germany. Bonhoeffer's brother was busy working with Albert Einstein and Max Planck splitting the atom. Other family members occupied various high-ranking positions in government and business. To say he was well-connected would be an enormous understatement, and Bonhoeffer viewed his connections as a stewardship responsibility. By 1938, he was considering how his connections could be used to defeat the Nazis. Ultimately, he decided to join his brother-in-law in the Abwehr, the German military intelligence organization. He used his position to serve the German resistance movement, attempting to actively dismantle the Nazi regime by working as a double agent until his arrest and martyrdom.

The story of Bonhoeffer offering the Hitler salute in the café was relayed by his friend and biographer Eberhard Bethge. Bethge was truly shocked when he saw Bonhoeffer offer the salute. But later, reflecting on the episode at the restaurant, he realized it was simply a result of Bonhoeffer's move from being a conscientious objector to the Nazis to being an active conspirator against them. As another of Bonhoeffer's biographers explains, "He didn't want to be thought of as an objector. He wanted to blend in. He didn't want to make an anti-Hitler statement; he had bigger fish to fry. He wanted to be left alone to do the things he knew God was calling him to do, and these things required him to remain unnoticed. . . . [Bonhoeffer] had crossed from 'confession' to 'resistance.'"[2]

With this backstory in mind, let's turn our attention to the spectrum of conviction developed in chapter two. Although Bonhoeffer and Schneider came from two different theological traditions (Lutheran and Reformed), their theological beliefs for our present purposes were largely the same. They shared a confessional belief that Jesus Christ was God incarnate and therefore the rightful Lord of every human life. They both believed that Jesus acts in human history both through providentially directing human affairs and also by calling individuals personally. They agreed that all human life was life in the image of God and worthy of protection. As we move to the right across the spectrum to moral mandates, they continue to agree with one another. Bonhoeffer and Schneider both immediately opposed the Nazi regime because of its dehumanizing practices toward Jews (as well as the Roma, persons with disabilities or mental illnesses, gay and lesbian persons, and a host of others) who were made in God's image and therefore people of full moral standing—neighbors whom they were called to love and protect. Both objected a few years later when the so-called "Aryan Clause" was passed. The Aryan Clause forbade people of Jewish heritage from serving as pastors. They saw the Aryan Clause as a violation of a moral mandate—a major step down a slippery slope of making Jewish people second-class citizens, and then not citizens at all, and finally creatures that had more in common with animals in general or vermin in particular than with their fellow human beings. Such beliefs, they felt, must be rejected by all Christians.

As we move on to core values, some very interesting differences begin to emerge. To illustrate the differences, it would help to include Martin Neimöller, a renowned Christian leader who also detested the Nazis and who had been appointed as the head of the Confessing Church. He is the author of the poem about neighbor love that we discussed in chapter 2. Niemöller, Schneider, and Bonhoeffer all stood together on issues of the full humanity of Jewish persons and therefore their equal standing before God and human law. However, on the implications of the gospel for human government, Niemöller was at odds with both Bonhoeffer and Schneider. A core value of Niemöller's included a prevalent teaching of Lutheranism that the church and state are two disjunctive kingdoms that do not answer to each other but rather each answers directly to God. Therefore, Niemöller was clearly opposed to the state meddling in church affairs (as the Nazis were prone to do), but he was equally opposed to the church meddling with the state. Though certainly no supporter of the Nazi regime, he was very reluctant to use the influence of the church to oppose secular government. He was not a coward—he was imprisoned in the Sachsenhausen and Dachau concentration camps for many years and narrowly escaped execution. But nonetheless, his core values regarding the relationship between church and state moderated his willingness to actively oppose the existing regime.

In contrast, Bonhoeffer and Schneider felt they were not only permitted to oppose the regime but obligated to do so. They opposed Nazi interference in church affairs (just as Niemöller did), but they also opposed Nazi laws and political policies. Indeed, Bonhoeffer's aborted radio address mentioned earlier was focused on the notion of the "Führer." This concept of governmental and cultural leadership had a long history in Germany, a history that Hitler expertly exploited. Bonhoeffer believed this concept of the Führer contained a misshapen understanding of the proper place of human leadership before God. The mistake was *political* and not regarding church affairs. Schneider, similarly, was quick to oppose Nazi policy at all levels—both ecclesial and political. In this, they both differed from Niemöller—a person they nonetheless admired and respected.

But there were some values even Bonhoeffer and Schneider differed on. Schneider placed a high value on obeying commands, and he tended to understand the lordship of Christ through this lens. Removing his cap for the Nazi flag was not simply wrong, it was a violation of the command not to commit idolatry. Honoring the Lord meant obeying his Word and letting the chips fall where they may. End of story. Similarly, the bond between pastor and church (shepherd and flock) was under the authority of the great shepherd; therefore he could not accept reassignment from the government.

Once he saw a specific biblical principle that addressed a matter, the matter was settled. If that meant imprisonment or death, so be it. Bonhoeffer viewed the lordship of Christ somewhat differently. As he put it, "when we come to Jesus, he bids us come and die,"[3] so he didn't soft-pedal the demands of following Christ. Indeed, he is famous for denouncing cheap grace, which does not demand true discipleship. But for Bonhoeffer, the lordship of Christ was more personal than legal; it was more a matter of obeying the commander rather than the commandment. For Bonhoeffer, his deeply personalized lordship commitment meant an absolute sense of calling about matters for which there was no command. So, for example, his return to Germany from the United States in 1939 was prompted by his strong personal call to stand or fall with his people. A few years later, Bonhoeffer's sense of calling compelled him to participate in active resistance to Hitler and the Nazi regime—including involvement in a secret conspiracy to assassinate Hitler that required him to remain unnoticed by the authorities as much as possible. Therefore, even if the Nazi salute was "idolatrous," it was necessary for the bigger task to which God had called him. Ultimately, a very subtle difference in the way in which Schneider and Bonhoeffer conceived of the lordship of Christ led to a very large difference in their personal guidelines for conduct.

So the spectrum of conviction helps us understand the differences between fellow Nazi resisters such as Niemöller, Schneider, and Bonhoeffer by seeing more clearly where the differences emerge. Schneider and Bonhoeffer also offer a good example of the possibility of having to separate over missional differences. Schneider advocated the "high road" of absolute rejection of any compromise or appearance of compromise. But Bonhoeffer saw things differently. His personal calling led him to pursue a course of active resistance that required him to fly below the radar and offer the Nazi salute or say "Heil Hitler" if the situation demanded it.

By contrast, Schneider was absolutely convinced that a faithful Christian must do the right thing and let the chips fall where they may. For Bonhoeffer, that course of action would guarantee that he would lose all of his chips long before he could actually play the hand that God had dealt him. Clearly, it would have been hard for them to work together. What would happen if they were meeting in a public place and Schneider refused to stand, or salute, or take off his cap? The suspicion of the Nazis would immediately fall upon the whole group, not just Schneider. Schneider was not wired for covert operations. It is easy to image that they would have to part ways for the sake of pursuing their respective missions.

Let's conclude this bit of history with an imaginary scenario. Suppose that Schneider's widow, Margarete, was visiting with a friend in East Prussia on the fateful day when France surrendered. Imagine the friend invited her to coffee on that sunny afternoon in order to comfort her in the midst of her grief over her husband's death in Buchenwald just a year earlier. Imagine she, too, was at the same café and heard the trumpet fanfare and then saw Bonhoeffer rise and offer the Nazi salute. Quite likely, she would be horrified. Finally, imagine she is sitting beside her friend in church the next week and the pastor introduces their special guest preacher, the esteemed Dietrich Bonhoeffer.

Would she get up and leave? Would she ask how the church could possibly welcome someone who so completely accommodated the Nazis? Perhaps she would ask how they could offer her condolences on her husband's martyrdom while at the very same time inviting Bonhoeffer to speak to the congregation. Imagine she asked Bethge what Bonhoeffer whispered in his ear. How would she feel if he told her that Bonhoeffer said, "Raise your arm! We'll have to run risks for many different things, but this silly salute is not one of them!" How would it feel for her to hear it called "a silly salute?" I'm sure she had many words to describe the salute for which her husband died, but I doubt that "silly" was one of them.

What if you were the pastor of the church in question. What would you say to Margarete Schneider? This is where the conviction spectrum can be helpful. One might be able to invite her into a serious conversation. Instead of starting the discussion with the "silly salute" (and I'm sure Bonhoeffer would not have used that phrase with Schneider's widow!), perhaps the discussion could begin by thickening the convictions—identifying the profound agreement between her husband and Bonhoeffer on defining Christian beliefs, as well as on the moral mandates that result from lordship of Christ over our personal lives. Furthermore, one could point out their shared rejection of the Nazi regime and their treatment of the Jews. It would also help to share some of Bonhoeffer's backstory, including the unique opportunities his family connections gave him. You could explain that Bonhoeffer understood his personal call as opposing the Nazi regime by direct action. And finally, you could share that in light of this missional difference, his personal calling would be immediately foreclosed if he made ongoing public opposition to the regime and refused to make daily acknowledgments like the Nazi salute or closing conversations with saying, "Heil Hitler." You could even convey the imminent danger in which Bonhoeffer found himself and the likelihood that he, too, would be martyred.

Would Margarete Schneider have understood these things at that moment?

I surely could not say. I would also be very understanding if she did not. However, those truths are actually there to be understood. Indeed, I would suggest that Schneider and Bonhoeffer offer a perfect example of deeply held but conflicting Christian convictions. It also offers a good example of the importance of evaluating one another's conduct only after we have understood how that person's conduct emerged from his or her confessional beliefs, moral mandates, and core values. Once we have done this, we may find we have far more that unites us than divides us, and that those things that unite us are actually the things that are of greatest importance. Perhaps Margarete Schneider could weep for her husband even as she prayed protection and success for Dietrich Bonhoeffer, who had been called to a profoundly different but equally challenging path of discipleship.

CONCLUSION

Is the Bible historically accurate?

In light of evolution, how can I still believe in a literal Adam and Eve?

Does it really matter if Jesus rose from the dead?

Is it crazy to assert that the Bible is God's definitive word to the world?

In the late 1950s traditional answers to these questions came under great scrutiny from not only secular experts but also Christians themselves. *Wouldn't it just be easier to think of the Bible as a collection of creative fictions that offer ancient wisdom?* Feeling the cultural ground shift from under them, many churches hunkered down on traditional answers and sought to weed out the unfaithful. But what if you had legitimate questions? Where could you go to process?

In 1955 Francis and Edith Schaeffer opened their home in Switzerland to any and all who had questions. They called their meeting place *L'Abri*, which is the French word for "shelter." Not only did it serve as a shelter from encroaching secularism, but it was a place where people could talk free of judgment and unproductive arguing. The idea caught on, and soon similar shelters opened across Europe and in the United States. Today, L'Abri is still thriving, with branches in Australia, Canada, England, United States, Korea, Switzerland, Brazil, and South Africa.

L'Abri was just the start of Francis Schaeffer's legacy. His books, such as *The God Who Is There*, *How Should We Then Live?*, *True Spirituality*, *Whatever Happened to the Human Race?*, and *The Great Evangelical Disaster* are standard reading at seminaries and Christian universities worldwide. In a time of encroaching theological liberalism, he helped found the International Council on Biblical Inerrancy. Today, Schaeffer is remembered as one of the most influential Christian thinkers of the twentieth century.

Yet, all of it almost didn't happen.

At the age of thirty-nine, before one book had been written or a single visitor arrived at L'Abri, Francis Schaeffer had a crisis of faith. "For the sake of honesty," confided Schaeffer to his wife, "I had to go all the way back to my agnosticism and think through the whole matter."[1] What prompted this reexamination of faith? Conflict with fellow Christians.

After witnessing a liberal shift in mainline denominations, Schaeffer and others created a separatist movement in protest. However, over time he became deeply concerned with how members of this fledgling movement acted toward those they opposed. Rather than angrily blasting those with whom they disagreed, "we could have remembered that, wrong though they are, they are for the most part brothers in Christ."[2] The vitriol directed at others eventually turned inward, and Schaeffer's movement was filled with infighting and verbal attacks against each other. Ironically, those within the separatist movement began separating from each other. The conflict among Christ followers sent him on a journey of self-doubt and introspection. In a personal letter, Schaeffer was nearly despondent as he asked, "the command to love should mean something?"[3]

Twenty years after his crisis of faith, Schaeffer was still wrestling with the question of what Christ's love should mean. Of the twenty-two books he'd write, Schaeffer identified his shortest book—a mere fifty pages—as his most important. In *The Mark of a Christian*, Schaeffer provocatively suggests that exhibiting Jesus' love will

either validate or invalidate our Christian witness: "Upon his [Jesus']
authority he gives the world the right to judge whether you and I
are born-again Christians on the basis of our observable love toward
all Christians."[4]

Living out our convictions is how we express our devotion to
Christ. However, if holding convictions makes us uncivil and ultimately unloving, we are forced to choose between devotion to our
beliefs and the unity of the body. And this is an intolerable choice.
We simply must find ways to deepen our beliefs and convictions
while preserving the unity of the Spirit and the bond of peace. If we
don't, two unacceptable results will follow. If civility is absent from
Christian communicators, an argument-saturated world will judge
us to be no different from anyone else. We will be Christians who
don't bear the mark of a Christian. A second tragic result will be
risking the loss of an upcoming generation of potential Francis
Schaeffers who believe that the command to love one another
should mean something, but upon looking around at their fellow
believers, they discover it does not. But, such results can be avoided.

The ancient writers of the book of Proverbs give us hope as they
assert that when our ways are pleasing to the Lord he "causes their
enemies to make peace with them" (Prov 16:7). What ways are
pleasing to God? We've suggested that, in part, seeking the forgotten middle ground, creating fences rather than divisions,
achieving authentic disagreements, avoiding placing people in
rigid categories, and showing love by carefully mapping a person's
convictions are all ways that please God. If these prompt even our
most ardent opponents to adopt a peaceful stance toward us, then
imagine how it will impact those we call brothers and sisters. In the
end, we may still disagree, but the mark of the Christian will be
evident to all.

ACKNOWLEDGMENTS

This book is part of a larger vision called the Winsome Conviction Project (WCP), which seeks to reintroduce civility and compassion back into our disagreements with both Christians and those outside our community. We have a passion to foster conversations that deepen relationships and enrich lives rather than tear us apart. But these conversations will be hard. We know our deeply held convictions will meet honest disagreements from others, so we must cultivate a virtuous communication climate in which participants care deeply, think clearly, speak graciously, and listen patiently. The WCP will be actively working to provide resources to make such conversations successful. Check out our website at winsomeconviction.com.

The WCP would not be possible without the generous support of two donor families—thank you for your constant encouragement and vision. Thank you to the brain trust of our project: Brian Shook, David Turner, and Crystal Tosello. Kevin Royce and Denise Migeot, thanks for all the attention you give to our efforts. Last, thank you to Al Hsu for going above and beyond the normal responsibilities of an editor; your keen insight and direction shaped our book.

We would also like to acknowledge the faculty, staff, and administration of Biola University. Not only were we able to use a sabbatical leave to complete writing this book and develop the WCP, we also have been given countless opportunities to test out these principles in both small groups and large, both in public and in private. As with any testing, it has been a learning experience, but we appreciate the grace, support, and persistence of our leadership in helping to make Biola University a good place to develop and communicate deeply held convictions, and live them out in a loving Christian community.

NOTES

INTRODUCTION

[1]Mark Galli, "Trump Should Be Removed from Office," *Christianity Today,* December 19, 2019, www.christianitytoday.com/ct/2019/december-web -only/trump-should-be-removed-from-office.html.

[2]Melissa Barnhart, "Nearly 200 Evangelical Leaders Slam Christianity Today for Questioning Their Christian Witness," *The Christian Post,* December 22, 2019, www.christianpost.com/news/nearly-200-evangelical -leaders-slam-christianity-today-for-questioning-their-christian-witness.html.

[3]If interested in following Tim's thought process, the InterVarsity Press books most relevant are *The God Conversation: Using Illustrations to Explain . Your Faith* (with J. P. Moreland), *Authentic Communication: Christian Speech Engaging Culture* (with Todd Lewis), *I Beg to Differ: Navigating Difficult Conversations with Truth and Love,* and *Winsome Persuasion: Christian Influence in a Post-Christian World* (with Rick Langer).

1. HISTORICAL PRELUDE: ROGER WILLIAMS

[1]Edwin S. Gaustad, *Liberty of Conscience: Roger Williams in America* (King of Prussia, PA: Judson Press, 1999), 26.

[2]Gaustad, *Liberty of Conscience,* 84.

[3]Gaustad, *Liberty of Conscience,* 84 (emphasis added).

[4]Lynch v. Donnelly, 465 U.S. 668 (1984), http://law2.umkc.edu/faculty /projects/ftrials/conlaw/lynch.html.

[5]Gaustad, *Liberty of Conscience*, 34.

[6]John Winthrop, *Winthrop's Journal*, "History of New England," 1630-1649 (New York: Charles Scribner's Sons, 1908), 1:316.

[7]John Cotton, ed., *John Cotton's Answer to Roger Williams (1647)*, vol. II, *Publications of the Narragansett Club* (Providence, RI: 1867), 55.

2. DISPUTABLE MATTERS: THE FORGOTTEN MIDDLE GROUND

[1]World Christian Database, https://worldchristiandatabase.org/.

[2]A short overview of Mennonite schisms is found in the Global Anabaptist Mennonite Encyclopedia Online, https://gameo.org/index.php?title =Schisms. Further details are found in many related articles on the same website. A helpful informal summary can be found at https:// elmiramennonitemartin.wordpress.com/2016/07/27/174.

[3]F. F. Bruce, *The Letter of Paul to the Romans: An Introduction and Commentary* (Grand Rapids, MI: Eerdmans, 1985), 239.

3. THE CONVICTION SPECTRUM

[1]Timothy Keller, "How Do Christians Fit into the Two-Party System? They Don't," *New York Times*, September 29, 2018, www.nytimes.com/2018 /09/29/opinion/sunday/christians-politics-belief.html.

[2]Joseph Cardinal Bernardin, *Consistent Ethic of Life: Joseph Cardinal Bernardin*, ed. Thomas G. Fuechtmann (Kansas City, MO: Sheed & Ward, 1988).

[3]Jonathan Haidt, *The Righteous Mind: Why Good People Are Divided by Politics and Religion* (New York: Pantheon Books, 2012).

[4]Shalom Schwartz, "An Overview of the Schwartz Theory of Basic Values," *Online Readings in Psychology and Culture* 2, no. 1 (2012), https://doi .org/10.9707/2307-0919.1116.

[5]*Holocaust Encyclopedia*, https://encyclopedia.ushmm.org/content/en /article/martin-niemoeller-first-they-came-for-the-socialists.

[6]Jennifer A. Herdt, "Christian Humility, Courtly Civility, and the Code of the Streets," *Modern Theology* 25, no. 4 (October 2009): 553.

[7]Herdt, "Christian Humility," 554.

4. DOES DIVISION HAVE TO BE DIVISIVE?

[1]A. F. Wall, "Gnosticism," in *The Zondervan Encyclopedia of the Bible: Revised Full-Color Edition*, ed. Moisés Silva and Merrill C. Tenney (Grand Rapids, MI: Zondervan Academic, 2010).

[2]I. Howard Marshall, *The Acts of the Apostles: An Introduction and Commentary* (Grand Rapids, MI: Eerdmans, 1980), 258.

[3]Fred Sanders, "18 Theses on the Father and the Son," The Scriptorum Daily, June 13, 2016, http://scriptoriumdaily.com/18-theses-on-the -father-and-the-son/.

5. CROSSCULTURAL INTERLUDE: OF TATTOOS AND ADULTERY

[1]Amy Mendina, "Is My Faith More Authentic Than Your Faith?" EFCA (blog), August 15, 2017, www.efca.org/blog/engaging-culture/my-faith -more-authentic-your-faith.

6. HOW UNITY IS THREATENED

[1]Clinton Arnold, *Ephesians* (Grand Rapids, MI: Zondervan, 2010), 31.

[2]Kenneth Wuest, *Word Studies in the Greek New Testament*, vol. 1 (Grand Rapids, MI: Eerdmans, 1973), 95.

[3]You can read my entry here: http://ccca.biola.edu/lent/2019/#day -mar-13.

[4]Wuest, *Word Studies in the Greek*, 95.

[5]Victor Turner, *Dramas, Fields, and Metaphors: Symbolic Action in Human Society* (Ithaca, NY: Cornell University Press, 1974), 38.

[6]Turner, *Dramas, Fields, and Metaphors*, 39.

[7]Imeyen Ebong, "Why Conflict Can Actually Be a Good Thing," *Forbes*, December 4, 2017, www.forbes.com/sites/baininsights/2017/12/04 /conflict-is-good/#71fdd6067efd.

[8]Turner, *Dramas, Fields, and Metaphors*, 39.

[9]Turner, *Dramas, Fields, and Metaphors*, 39.

[10]Nicole Roccas, *Time and Despondency: Regaining the Present in Faith and Life* (Chesterton, IN: Ancient Faith Publishing, 2017), 58.

[11]Michael Papa, Tom Daniels, and Barry Spiker, *Organizational Communication: Perspectives and Trends* (Los Angeles: Sage Publications, 2008), 216.

[12]Turner, *Dramas, Fields, and Metaphors*, 41.

[13]J. T. O'Donnell, "HR Is Not Your Friend. Here's Why," Inc., accessed January 13, 2020, https://www.inc.com/jt-odonnell/what-20-somethings -need-to-know-about-complaining-to-hr.html.

[14]See also: 1 Tim. 3:1-13, 2 Tim. 2:1-13, Acts 6:1-6, and Ex. 18:21-22. While these passages specifically mention qualifications for male leadership, we acknowledge that these qualifications can also apply to women who assume leadership roles or serve in HR departments. Scriptures and

church history record that the early church employed deaconesses who, in part, helped serve the sacraments.

[15]Turner, *Dramas, Fields, and Metaphors*, 41.

[16]Our premise can work equally well at a Christian university or company. While it's totally within the purview of an employee to disagree with management and utilize all appropriate avenues (e.g., human resources department, faculty senate), once a decision is rendered one must determine if he or she can abide by it. No doubt, this will require determining if one's views of the issue are a matter of absolutes.

7. PERCEPTION IS REALITY

[1]To further explore see: G. A. Quattrone, "On the Congruity Between Internal States and Actions," *Psychological Bulletin*, 1985, 98, 3-40.

[2]Richard Alleyne, "Welcome to the Information Age—174 Newspapers a Day," February 11, 2011, www.telegraph.co.uk/news/science/science-news/8316534/Welcome-to-the-information-age-174-newspapers-a-day.html.

[3]"Can We Trust First Impressions," Psychologies, January 4, 2012, www.psychologies.co.uk/self/can-we-trust-first-impressions.html.

[4]Thank you to Al Hsu for this observation.

[5]Carol Kuruvilla, "Alexandria Ocasio-Cortez: Jesus Would Be Maligned as 'Radical' by Today's Congress," February 27, 2020, www.huffpost.com/entry/alexandria-ocasio-cortez-faith_n_5e580e16c5b6450a30bbd0f7.

[6]Maeve McDermott, "Taylor Swift Has Angered Many People with Her 'You Need to Calm Down' Release. Here's Why," *USA Today,* June 21, 2019, www.usatoday.com/story/life/music/2019/06/21/how-taylor-swift-angered-everyone-you-need-calm-down/1512715001.

[7]Maria Lugones, "Playfulness, 'World-traveling,' and Loving Perception," in D. Soyini Madison, ed. *The Woman that I Am: The Literature and Culture of Contemporary Women of Color* (New York: St. Martin's Press, 1994), 631.

[8]Lugones, "Playfulness, 'World-traveling,' and Loving Perception," 631.

[9]Lugones, "Playfulness, 'World-traveling,' and Loving Perception," 632.

[10]To read the stories of those who seek to embrace both evangelicalism and evolution see: *How I Changed my Mind about Evolution: Evangelicals Reflect on Faith and Science*, Kathryn Applegate and J. B. Stump, eds. (Downers Grove, IL: IVP Academic, 2016). To consider a recent rebuttal to an openness to evolution see: *Theistic Evolution: A Scientific, Philosophical, and Theological Critique.* J. P. Moreland, Stephen C. Meyer,

Christopher Shaw, Ann K. Gauger and Wayne Grudem, eds. (Wheaton, IL: Crossway, 2017).

[11]Todd Charles Wood and Darrel R. Falk, *The Fool and the Heretic: How Two Scientists Moved Beyond Labels to a Christian Dialogue about Creation and Evolution* (Grand Rapids, MI: Zondervan, 2019), 43.

[12]Wood and Falk, *The Fool and the Heretic*, 169.

[13]Wood and Falk, *The Fool and the Heretic*, 46.

[14]Wood and Falk, *The Fool and the Heretic*, 85.

[15]Wood and Falk, *The Fool and the Heretic*, 87.

[16]Wood and Falk, *The Fool and the Heretic*, 88.

[17]Wood and Falk, *The Fool and the Heretic*, 88.

[18]Wood and Falk, *The Fool and the Heretic*, 88.

[19]Wood and Falk, *The Fool and the Heretic*, 93.

[20]Wood and Falk, *The Fool and the Heretic*, 89.

[21]Wood and Falk, *The Fool and the Heretic*, 89.

[22]Eugene Peterson, *Subversive Spirituality* (Grand Rapids, MI: Eerdmans, 1997), 189.

[23]Wood and Falk, *Fool and the Heretic*, 172.

8. FELLOWSHIP GROUPS OR ECHO CHAMBERS?

[1]Lawrence Fry, "Applied Communication Research on Group Facilitation in Natural Settings," in *Innovations in Group Facilitation: Applications in Natural Settings*, ed. Lawrence Fry (Cresskill, NJ: Hampton Press, 1995), 5.

[2]While Dunbar views these findings through an evolutionary lens, his research has strong implications for how a community segments itself. Even as many will reject his theoretical starting point, his insights are well worth considering. To read more: Robin I. M. Dunbar, "The Social Brain Hypothesis," *Evolutionary Anthropology* 6 (1998): 178-190.

[3]Lisa Beach, "How to Manage Expectations for Your Friendships," *USA Today*, September 1, 2019, www.usatoday.com/story/life/2019/09/01/ways-nurture-friendships/2129538001.

[4]Tom Foreman, "Analysis: The Race Factor in George Zimmerman's Trial," CNN, July 15, 2013, www.cnn.com/2013/07/14/justice/zimmerman-race-factor/index.html?hpt=hp_t1.

[5]Foreman, "Analysis: The Race Factor."

[6]Sherry Turkel, *Alone Together: Why We Expect More from Technology and Less from Each Other* (New York: Basic Books, 2011), 176.

[7]Kathrin Lassila, "A Brief History of Groupthink," *Yale Alumni Magazine,* January/February 2008, https://yalealumnimagazine.com/articles /1947-a-brief-history-of-groupthink.

[8]Tom Nichols, *The Death of Expertise: The Campaign against Established Knowledge and Why it Matters* (New York: Oxford University Press, 2017), 3.

[9]Tomas Chamorro-Premuzic, "How the Web Distorts Reality and Impairs Our Judgement Skills," *Guardian,* May 13, 2014, www.theguardian .com/media-network/media-network-blog/2014/may/13/internet -confirmation-bias.

[10]Sadly, harsh pronouncements about Reformed theology often go unchallenged in the writings of Arminians or at non-Reformed seminaries.

[11]Megan Phelps-Roper, "I Grew Up in the Westboro Baptist Church. Here's Why I Left," TED, March 6, 2017, www.youtube.com/watch?v =bVV2Zk88beY.

[12]William Cummings, "Obama Warns Democrats That Ideological 'Rigidity' Can Lead to a 'Circular Firing Squad,'" *USA Today,* April 8, 2019, www .usatoday.com/story/news/politics/elections/2019/04/08/2020-election -barack-obama-warns-democrats-circular-firing-squad/3398051002.

[13]John Stott, *The Message of Ephesians. God's New Society* (Downers Grove, IL: InterVarsity Press, 1979), 172.

[14]Ryan Denison, "John MacArthur Tells Beth Moore 'Go Home': 3 Ways to Disagree Better," Christian Headlines, October 23, 2019, www .christianheadlines.com/columnists/denison-forum/john-macarthur -tells-beth-moore-go-home-3-ways-to-disagree-better.html.

[15]Douglass Stone & Sheila Heen, *Thanks for the Feedback: The Science and Art of Receiving Feedback Well* (New York: Penguin Books, 2014), 8.

[16]Roger Fisher and William Ury, *Getting to Yes: Negotiating Agreement Without Giving In* (New York: Penguin Books, 1991), 24.

9. POWER AND CIVILITY IN A BROKEN SOCIETY

[1]Marva Dawn, *Powers, Weakness, and the Tabernacling of God* (Grand Rapids, MI: Eerdmans, 2001). See especially chapter 1.

[2]Julia T. Wood, *Gendered Lives: Communication, Gender and Culture,* 11th ed. (Stamford, CT: Cengage Learning, 2015), 280.

[3]Geert Hofstede, *Culture's Consequences: International Differences in Work-related Values* (Newbury, CA: Sage, 1984), 30.

[4]Rebecca Konyndyk DeYoung, *Glittering Vices: A New Look at the Seven Deadly Sins and Their Remedies* (Grand Rapids, MI: Brazos Press, 2009), 118 (emphasis in original).

[5]DeYoung, *Glittering Vices*, 122.

[6]Clint Arnold, *Ephesians: Exegetical Commentary on the New Testament* (Grand Rapids, MI: Zondervan, 2010), 307.

[7]Arnold, *Ephesians: Exegetical Commentary*, 308.

[8]DeYoung, *Glittering Vices*, 130.

[9]Benjamin DeMott, "Seduced by Civility: Political Manners and the Crisis of Democratic Values," *The Nation* 263, no. 19 (December 6, 1996): 16.

[10]DeMott, "Seduced by Civility," 14.

[11]Michael Arceneaux, "I Respect You Immensely, Barack Obama, But I Don't Need Lessons about 'Being Woke' and 'Cancel Culture,'" *Independent*, October 30, 2019, www.independent.co.uk/voices/obama-woke -meaning-michelle-cancel-culture-foundation-chicago-a9178436.html (emphasis added).

[12]Suzanna Walters, "Why Can't We Hate Men?" *Washington Post*, June 8, 2018, www.washingtonpost.com/opinions/why-cant-we-hate-men/2018 /06/08/f1a3a8e0-6451-11e8-a69c-b944de66d9e7_story.html.

[13]Howard Thurman, *Jesus and the Disinherited* (Boston, MA: Beacon Press, 1996), 78.

[14]Stephen Carter, *Civility: Manners, Morals, and the Etiquette of Democracy* (New York: Basic Books, 1998), 35.

[15]John Perkins, *With Justice for All: A Strategy for Community Development* (Ada, MI: Baker Books, 2014), 27.

[16]Carter, *Civility*, 279-285.

[17]Marilynne Robinson, *Gilead* (New York: Picador, 2006), 124.

10. HEALING JOINT PAIN IN THE BODY OF CHRIST

[1]Rebecca Konyndyk DeYoung, *Glittering Vices: A New Look at the Seven Deadly Sins and Their Remedies* (Grand Rapids, MI: Brazos Press, 2009), 137.

[2]DeYoung, *Glittering Vices*, 137.

[3]C. S. Lewis, *Mere Christianity* (San Francisco: HarperOne, 2015), 128, emphasis ours.

[4]DeYoung, *Glittering Vices*, 138.

[5]"Where We Stand," AND Campaign, accessed March 12, 2020, https:// andcampaign.org/where-we-stand.

[6]Marilynne Robinson, *Gilead* (New York: Picador, 2006), 81 (emphasis added).

[7]Thabiti Anyabwile, "Can We Talk? Or, Why I Think a Trump Presidency Is Intolerable Even Though You Might Not Agree," TGC, June 6, 2016, www.thegospelcoalition.org/blogs/thabiti-anyabwile/can-we-talk -or-why-i-think-a-trump-presidency-is-intolerable-even-though-you-might -not-agree (emphasis in original).

[8]Anyabwile.

[9]Peter T. Coleman, *The Five Percent [Electronic Resource]: Finding Solutions to Seemingly Impossible Conflicts*, 1st ed. (New York: PublicAffairs, 2011), 3-4.

11. CONVICTION MAPPING

[1]Roger Fisher and Daniel Shapiro, *Beyond Reason: Using Emotions as You Negotiate* (New York: Penguin Books, 2005), 5.

[2]"'Ok Boomer': Apathy, Anger and a Viral Meme," 1A, November 7, 2019, www.npr.org/2019/11/07/777296535/ok-boomer-apathy-anger -and-a-viral-meme.

[3]To read more of this study and others, see Sonja Lyubomirsky, *The How of Happiness: A New Approach to Getting the Life You Want* (New York, NY: Penguin Books, 2007).

[4]Justin Brierly, *Unbelievable? Why, After Ten Years of Talking with Atheists, I'm Still a Christian* (London: Society for Promoting Christian Knowledge, 2017), 124.

[5]Brierly, *Unbelievable?*, 127.

[6]Brierly, *Unbelievable?*, 177.

[7]"What's Pulling America Apart?" CNN, February 3, 2019, www.cnn.com /videos/opinions/2019/11/11/america-political-divide-orig.cnn.

[8]Emma Green, "These Are the Americans Who Live in a Bubble," *Atlantic*, February 21, 2019, www.theatlantic.com/politics/archive/2019/02 /americans-remain-deeply-ambivalent-about-diversity/583123/.

12. GUIDELINES FOR HARD CONVERSATIONS

[1]Maya Hampton, "Fenced-in Playgrounds: How Boundaries Can Encourage Greater Creativity," Medium, October 25, 2019, https://uxdesign.cc /fenced-in-playgrounds-d5f9371f8414.

13. HISTORICAL POSTLUDE: CONVICTIONS IN NAZI GERMANY

[1]"The Buchenwald Letters, III," *Leben: A Journal of Reformation Life* (blog), December 19, 2016, https://leben.us/buchenwald-letters-iii.

[2]Eric Metaxas, *Bonhoeffer: Pastor, Martyr, Prophet, Spy* (Nashville: Thomas Nelson, 2011), 362.

[3]Dietrich Bonhoeffer, *The Cost of Discipleship* (New York: Scribner, 1963), 99.

CONCLUSION

[1]Lane T. Dennis, *Letters of Francis A. Schaeffer* (Westchester, IL: Good News Publishing, 1985), 12.

[2]Dennis, *Letters of Francis A. Schaeffer*, 39.

[3]Dennis, *Letters of Francis A. Schaeffer*, 39.

[4]Francis A. Schaeffer, *The Mark of a Christian* (Downers Grove, IL: InterVarsity Press, 1970), 22.

NAME INDEX

SUBJECT INDEX